T0227476

A PRACTICAL GUIDE TO INDIE GAME MARKETING

A PRACTICAL GUIDE TO INDIE GAME MARKETING

JOEL DRESKIN

CRC Press
Taylor & Francis Group
Boca Raton London New York

CRC Press is an imprint of the
Taylor & Francis Group, an **Informa** business

CRC Press
Taylor & Francis Group
6000 Broken Sound Parkway NW, Suite 300
Boca Raton, FL 33487-2742

First issued in hardback 2017

ISBN-13: 978-1-138-80154-7 (pbk)
ISBN-13: 978-1-138-42823-2 (hbk)

Library of Congress Cataloging in Publication Data
An application for this title has been submitted

Typeset in Minion Pro
by Apex CoVantage, LLC

**Visit the Taylor & Francis Web site at
http://www.taylorandfrancis.com**

**and the CRC Press Web site at
http://www.crcpress.com**

Contents

1 Introduction   1

2 Marketing Fundamentals   5

3 Branding   21
   Written by Guest Author Tom Byron
   Case Study: Klei Entertainment   32

4 Developing Your Marketing Campaign and Calendar   35

5 Marketing Vehicles That Can Work Well for Indies   45
   Case Study: Supergiant Games   53

6 Developing the Marketing Plan   57
   Case Study: The Binary Mill's *Mini Motor Racing*   64

7 PR   69
   Written by Guest Author Emily Morganti
   Case Study: Additional PR Examples   92

8 Marketing Materials   101

9 Audience/Community Development   117
   Case Study: Telltale Games   127

10 Post-Launch   131
   Case Study: Flippfly's *Race the Sun*   138

11 What If Something Goes Wrong?!   143

Appendix One: Glossary   147

Appendix Two: Marketing Fundamentals Worksheet   151

Appendix Three: Marketing Plan Outline   155

Appendix Four: Checklists   159

Appendix Five: Press Release Worksheet   163

Index   167

Acknowledgments

Special thanks to friends, family, content reviewers, indies, marketers and games that have helped in the creation and inspiration for this book. And to Evan Washington, for bringing full color to the cover illustration.

Chapter 1
Introduction

Welcome!

Welcome to *A Practical Guide to Indie Game Marketing*! "Practical Guide" is a central principle driving the approach to this book. These pages provide tools and tactics for marketing your indie games, drawn from game marketing plans, case studies and seasoned industry veterans.

Marketing is nearly as critical for new indies' success as the games themselves. This book focuses on providing insights, key concepts and tools for effectively building visibility and interest in your games—whether you choose to market them yourself, hire specialists, work with agencies or sign with publishers.

Who Is This Book For?

- Individuals and indie teams developing games for consumers.
- Individuals and teams considering a move into the indie world—perhaps currently employed with larger gaming studios.
- Students thinking about going indie for their game releases—after they graduate or perhaps for school projects.

Regardless of the path you take to market, this book will help with the process of formulating and executing effective marketing plans.

How This Book Is Presented and Organized

The book begins with core fundamental concepts and provides pointers on when and how to start. It will assist with marketing terminology and key principles, while presenting information in regular speak, rather than buzzwords—keeping jargon to a minimum.

In approaching the book's organization and presentation, the publisher and author have designed for skimmability, opening each chapter with objective summaries and tip callouts and progressing to deeper information later on. The book includes numerous examples from real-world game launches and marketing materials, with a focus on those that have worked best.

Readers will come to this book with differing levels of marketing experience—a key reason we've taken this approach of designing for skimmability—so you can find the sections most relevant to you and skip over topics you're more familiar with. That said, I recommend spending time with the opening chapters. Some of you may have bypassed these fundamental planning and organizational steps in the past, but they can deliver tremendous benefits.

Following the initial sections on core concepts and getting started, the book provides chapters that focus on these important areas:

- Developing your marketing plan.
- Determining which kinds of programs you'll include in your plans, such as PR, advertising, promotions and others.
- Designing effective marketing materials—trailers, store pages, icons and more.
- Additional topics, such as developing your audience and post-launch programs.

About the Author

I work as an independent marketer, having built up experience at numerous companies in the San Francisco Bay area, including the LucasArts division of Lucasfilm, Telltale Games, and Macromedia (now Adobe). Earlier in my career, I worked in licensing and merchandising at Paramount Pictures, as well as advertising agencies. Projects I've driven have included big budget TV campaigns (one of which featured the real Jedi Starfighter from *Star Wars Episode II*), online, print and social media-centric programs, as well as smaller, grassroots initiatives. These launches have spanned many different platforms and channels—console, mobile, and desktop; digital and retail.

For a number of projects, I've taken approaches from larger companies and adapted them for organizations with different staff and budget sizes. As an example, I've helped conceive and run events that bring together indie studios with media and industry attendees for focused mixers and junkets. You can learn more at www.theindiemarketer.com.

Two chapters in this book feature contributions from special guest authors Tom Byron and Emily Morganti, writing enthusiastically on topics where they've established expertise: Branding and PR, respectively.

Let's Get Started!

Breaking down the basics and potential players for your game provides a great starting point for your plan. Chapter 2 provides guidelines on where, when and how to begin.

Chapter 2
Marketing Fundamentals

Marketing can be as essential for the success of your game as the game itself. Poor planning or neglect with marketing can kill an indie studio's dreams just as much as a sloppy approach to development. Some look at marketing as a task they should probably get to at some point. Too often, they never dive into it at all, or get to it very late in the process as an afterthought—and then might not consider the absence of marketing as a key factor if the game underperforms. Some might decide to skip marketing completely, believing they don't have the budget to support their games. Some want to believe that they don't need marketing because their game will sell itself.

Developers and aspiring studios that want to make games for a living and continue as indies should do everything they can to achieve these goals, including marketing! Successful marketing can provide a strong foundation for your studio's ongoing growth and for sharing your creations with as many people as possible. And you don't need a huge budget.

Strong marketing programs don't work like a standard kit, one-size-fits-all or checklist. Effective executions will vary significantly from one game to the next—based on the gameplay style, kinds of players, platforms, release timing, your goals, and much more.

Chapter Objectives:
- Determining how and when to begin the marketing planning process for your game.
- Identifying important key questions and considerations to address early on.

Where to Start

Since you're holding this book (even if you're just browsing in a store right now) you hopefully buy in to the importance of marketing. Here are some helpful starting points in approaching this for your game.

Marketing Fundamentals

Since marketing can be so broad and vast and can vary considerably from game to game, you'll find it helpful to begin with a shortlist of key concepts. This chapter frames these as "Marketing Fundamentals"—core building blocks that provide a starting point and help shape how you approach marketing for your game. Whether you decide to market the game yourself, with associates, or with a publisher responsible for marketing, you'll find it helpful to get a clear focus on these areas early on.

Description: What Is This Game?

Start by writing up a concise statement about your game, which many refer to as the "elevator pitch" (how you might describe your game in the time it takes for a typical elevator ride). This statement communicates the game concept as precisely as possible to a new person in two to three sentences, capturing its essence and characteristics that make it interesting and compelling. You can't really begin to build interest and appeal for a game with others until you zero in on the core attributes that make it most distinctive and can communicate them effectively.

Don't worry about crafting the perfect verbiage right away or trying to come up with the most clever tagline ever. This is a surefire path to writer's block. You'll likely tune and refine the wording many times before you begin presenting the statement to real prospective customers or partners. You might start with jotting down representative words, statements or bullet points about your game, write it out in longer form and prune it back until you get to its essence. Make sure you land at a place that's unique to your game—it shouldn't be so broad that it could refer to any number of different games out there.

> **Tip:** When writing your first brief game description, start by just getting words down on paper. Don't expect to create the most perfect, brilliant, awe-inspiring line with your first pass (this approach would most likely lead only to writer's block or a brain cramp!).

Here's one example of a game description. Can you guess the game?

A puzzle game where seven different types of colored blocks continuously fall from above and you must arrange them to make horizontal rows of bricks. Completing any row causes those blocks to disappear and the rest above to move downwards. The blocks above gradually fall faster and the game is over when the screen fills up and blocks can no longer fall from the top.

A shorter elevator pitch version of this description might read:

Race against the clock to match and arrange vertically falling colored blocks before they stack too high and fill the screen!

Positioning: Identifying an Appropriate Place for Your Game

Positioning definition: "an organized system for finding a window into the mind."[1]

Basically, this refers to how you position your game against others in your target market, how your game might compare or differ from others. You may hear some refer to "differentiators" in this context.

Positioning statements take the form of a single sentence (possibly two) that describes your game's primary appeal in relation to where it stands in the market. Positioning statements are succinct and speak to the main characteristics that make your game unique and interesting to potential customers. Again, think in terms of the market landscape—games that have preceded it, the genre, games that are anticipated around this game's release time—to frame the position you see your game occupying.

> **Tip:** As a test, ask yourself if your game's positioning statement could apply to other games—past, current or upcoming. If so, look for ways to improve upon your positioning statement wording, or possibly your approach to the game!

The marketing copy for *Super Meat Boy* includes a line that clearly captures the style of game and its unique position—based largely on the creators' rich imagination and brand of humor:

> "*Super Meat Boy is a tough-as-nails platformer where you play as an animated cube of meat who's trying to save his girlfriend (who happens to be made of bandages) from an evil fetus in a jar wearing a tux.*"

Positioning Statement vs. Tagline

Note that positioning statements are not typically taglines. Taglines are punchy, compelling one-liners that capture interest and help with selling the game. That said, a positioning statement can help generate a tagline, as well as other marketing materials and messaging. The outside world would typically not see a positioning statement. The outside world will see a tagline—in a trailer, an ad, marketing copy, etc.

Here are a few examples of real-world taglines from gaming— some for indies, others for larger releases. The column on the right side in the table below reverse engineers a positioning statement that might have led to this tagline.

Table 2.1 Sample Taglines and Positioning Statements

Tagline	Related Positioning Statement (author approximation)
If it's in the game, it's in the game! *EA Sports*	The most true-to-life sports game experience available—delivering all the thrills, details and nuances that make the sport exciting.
We're going to have fun . . . with science. *Portal 2*	Irreverent first person action puzzler, in a pseudoscientific setting. It's fun and funny, with personality and attitude.
Terror. Violence. Madness. Bedlam. A holiday paradise gone mad. *Dead Island*	Intense action RPG, where a zombie outbreak turns a tropical island vacation escape into an unfathomable nightmare!
Giant robots are menacing the City of Boston. Can you and your jetpack save us all? *Drunken Robot Pornography*	Wild and vivid, adrenaline-fueled first-person action game, juiced up with personality and flavor from the Boston-based developer.
Retro-futuristic drugstep arcade shooter. *Intake*	Extremely visual, color-infused arcade action game for today's gamers, inspired and influenced by great games of years past.

Unique Selling Proposition (USP): What Makes This Game So Special?

Some marketers identify a unique selling proposition (USP) in the early stages of their marketing plan development. Ideally, a USP answers the "so what?" question: What makes this game special?

Here's a useful USP definition:[2]

- The game makes a unique proposition to potential players—not merely hyperbole or empty words. The game marketing materials say: "Get this game, for *this specific reason.*"

- Others don't (and can't) offer this same proposition. It's completely unique.
- The proposition must be compelling in order to drive interest and, ultimately, players to your game.

The USP calls for a certain level of candor: Your game may not be the "ultimate" anything, the "best ever" or "unique" just because that's your intended goal. As a best practice, you should be clear on the USP even before you actually create the game. Ask yourself, what will make it truly compelling? What will make it stand out? What will make it special? *What will make people want to play it?* This kind of honest self-assessment at the early stages of your project can make a huge difference throughout the production process for the game you ultimately decide to create.

Developing Your Marketing Fundamentals

In addition to, and in support of, the communication and messaging concepts already covered here, your marketing fundamentals should include the following:

Style of Game

While traditional game genres help, as shorthand terminology for conveying a game play style, they have limitations at times too.

Some developers will create games that clearly fall into a specific genre: fighter, platformer, first-person shooter, etc. Some will have genre mixes that fit reasonably well for their game, such as action-RPG, sports-sim, etc. Be thoughtful on how and if you should use genre shorthand for describing your game. These terms can sometimes convey different ideas about the game than you're intending.

Alternatively, you can use different terms for describing your game than standard genre categories—for example, referring to a "story-driven" or "character-rich" experience, or a compelling, completely new kind of variation.

Note that as the game approaches release time, the distribution channel will likely ask for a genre categorization for placing the game in a relevant section of their store.

Target Audience

Who do you think this game is for? Who do you want it to be for? Is it for a fairly serious gamer who plays multiple hours, every day of the week? Or is it for a person who might only play a few times a week or month? Is it intended as a "five-minute game" for someone to pass the time when they're waiting in line or for a friend to get ready?

What's the expected age of the player? Teens? Early 20s? Younger kids? Is it intended for females more than males, or vice versa?

Don't give in to the temptation to say "I'm making such a great game, it's for everyone!" By defining the intended players clearly in advance, you can make the best game possible for these people. This also helps direct your communication programs in ways that can reach the very best prospects for the game, rather than an overly broad, poorly defined mass.

Some games have found their core players in different ways. For example, the developers will share prototypes and concepts with different groups and determine what kinds of players they appeal to most.

The Four "Ps"

Traditional marketing terminology refers to the "four Ps": product, price, promotion and place. These have been common framing principles for marketers and instructors for years.

- **Product:** What is the game, who is it for, what makes it most unique/interesting/compelling, what is its essence?
- **Price:** While the term "price" is self-explanatory, landing on your final price point(s) can involve a number of different considerations—for example, whether it's intended as a quick, inexpensive impulse purchase on mobile; a premium-priced deep, console experience; or possibly something completely different.
- **Promotion:** While developing your marketing plan, you'll determine which key vehicles, tactics and programs you'll use to promote your game. Will you focus on PR or building interest through word of mouth, social media or advertising? This is a core topic throughout the book.

- **Place:** The places you'll sell your game (different digital or possibly retail channels) play a central role in your game's viability and performance and the approach you take to marketing.

Release Timing

You'll want to determine what release timing will work best for you, while also assessing relevant advantages and disadvantages of different dates. For example:

Seasonality: 50% to 60% of game revenues for the calendar year typically come in the October through December holiday months. While this can be extremely lucrative for some, the entire industry consciously factors this into their plans as well. October through December not only have very high quantities of game releases, but also many of the biggest AAA games of the year release during these months. For this reason, building interest for your game at this time of year can be challenging. This isn't to say that indies should always steer clear of October through December. All should, however, incorporate this information into final launch date decisions when determining release dates.

> **Tip:** Pay close attention to external factors when mapping out marketing, announcement and launch plans—big holidays, events, other notable games, etc.

You should investigate additional timing and seasonality factors for different release dates as well—looking at big industry events (such as E3), holidays for major markets (July 4, Christmas), national or international events (political elections, the Olympics), and so on. You can look for opportunities to have these work in your favor (for example, topical content for a fall/Halloween release) or steer clear of a specific release date like December 31/January 1, acknowledging the difficulty of capturing attention for a new game release during this hectic, travel-heavy time of year.

Other Game Releases: Be sure to research expected release dates for other games while determining your final launch plans, particularly for games with similarities to your style of play and/or major new AAA releases from large publishers.

Timing for Different Platform Releases and Channels: You can benefit tremendously from planning to launch on multiple platforms and channels simultaneously. With this approach, you can maximize the game's potential sales by having it available in as many places as possible, to accommodate the platform preferences of different gamers. Also, the outreach, awareness and momentum you're generating can reap rewards across multiple systems.

Alternatively, when you have staggered launches, with varied dates on different platforms, you need to field multiple launch campaigns. Each subsequent launch typically does not carry the same impact as the first.

That said, an indie may not have resources and time available to manage multiple simultaneous platform releases. Staggered launches can and certainly have worked for some. We're highlighting these points here as additional central considerations for your release plan decision process.

Financials

Importantly, you'll need to determine the amount of funds you'll allocate for your marketing spending. While some would like this amount to be zero, that's not really realistic. Determining your marketing budget based on the amount remaining in your bank account (or credit line) isn't an ideal approach either. By the same token, those with more money available wouldn't maximize their sales simply by throwing lots of dollars at poorly conceived programs.

There are a variety of approaches to marketing that can work effectively, at relatively low costs. This book will provide guidelines to help in identifying which might fit best for your game. The following numbers will help you calculate the amount you should allocate for your game's marketing budget:

Your game development budget amount

Calculate your development budget based on hard costs and/or estimates of time invested by you and team members.

Use a reasonable hourly rate for your team members' time, multiplied by real hours dedicated to the project.

Your game's revenue goals—good, better, best

Determine revenue goals, based on your game's expected price multiplied by unit sales projections, and also estimate relevant deductions (for channel/distributors, publishers, etc.). It can help to have a low, medium and high target to provide a framework for your planning.

Table 2.2 Mini Financial Model

	Notes
Anticipated Game Revenues	Recommend Low, Medium, High scenarios
- Subtract Development Budget	
- Subtract Marketing Budget	Recommend Low, Medium, High scenarios
= Projected Profit / Loss	

Do you have minimum profit needs and/or desired income?

If you're willing/able to take a loss for this game, be clear on the acceptable loss you can absorb before you get into your marketing budget planning—and keep this number in view as you work through the process.

As a point of reference, some recommend allocating 8% to 15% of total revenues as a projected marketing budget amount. Note that this is typically used by larger organizations, and even in those cases, this calculation isn't intended to suggest a rigid adherence to a mathematic formula for the final budget decision. You shouldn't necessarily spend to the budget limit, if all dollars won't get spent intelligently, or flatly reject compelling marketing spending opportunities beyond your initial allocation.

Paths to Marketplace

You'll also need to decide early on how you'll bring your game to market. Some decide to sign with a publisher and others self-publish. Additionally, you can consider a variety of different approaches to staffing your marketing programs, or do it completely yourself.

Publisher vs. Self-Publishing

While the channels for self-publishing should continue to become more and more accessible—particularly through digital storefronts—some will choose to go with a publisher for releasing their games.

Some key considerations for signing with a publisher vs. self-publishing:

Table 2.3a Publisher vs. Self-Publishing

Publisher	Potential Benefits
Distribution	Publishers typically have distribution agreements in place with channels, facilitating the release process for games. Some publishers have particularly strong relationships with key channels, which can also help with securing high visibility for games at the storefront and periodic promotions.

Marketing	Publishers' marketing departments can take care of advertising, PR, trailer production, graphic design for key art and icons, trade shows and more.
	    With some publishers, games can benefit from cross-marketing programs in connection with different titles in their catalog.
	    The marketing spending budget would also come from the publisher, rather than from your own pocket.

Financials	You can reduce your financial risk by signing with a publisher. Publishers will typically offer a lump sum payment up front, in addition to taking on the marketing costs. In exchange, the developer gets a lower percentage of the game's per unit revenues than they would if they self-published.
Experience	Indies can gain from the experience of the publisher's team during the game launch process.

Table 2.3b Publisher vs. Self-Publisher

Self-Publishing	Potential Benefits
Brand development	Through self-publishing, you have the ability to establish a brand for your studio, which you can build over time. With a publisher, the developer's identity can get buried.
Control	You maintain full control over all elements of your game by self-publishing—how it's presented and showcased, down to the smallest details. In addition to driving the look and feel of marketing materials and PR, some publishers might want to get involved with game content, features, naming and more.
Financials	Rather than splitting revenues with both the distribution channel and publisher, you can increase your total income through self-publishing by eliminating a publisher cut.

Financial proposals from publishers can vary significantly—from 25% of net revenues to the developer and upwards, which can significantly impact your studio's earning potential—particularly after factoring in distribution channel fees, taxes and other possible unexpected costs.

Your Decision

Ultimately, you'll need to determine the most important priorities for your studio. You might want to consider a mix—going with a publisher for one game and self-publishing another.

Be sure to proceed with due diligence on possible publishers when making your decision. Talk to other developers that have distributed with them, check out their reputations and assess how well they present other games in their portfolio, how reliable they've been with paying out earnings due to developers, the specific marketing program commitments they'll make for published games and other possible considerations. You may certainly hear cautionary tales of publishers that sign many games to create a catalog, but do not ultimately provide sufficient attention or support to individual games as they approach their release dates. For agreements with publishers, you should pursue as much flexibility as possible, so that you do not relinquish important options and rights (intellectual property, future distribution rights for new platforms and sequels, etc.).

Marketing Staffing

Should You Do It Yourself?

There have been numerous indies that have chosen to self-market their games and been very effective. With PR in particular, the personal approach can often work well—with game developers telling their stories directly to journalists, speaking about their inspirations, and being themselves!

As these developers have shown, self-marketing is possible—and this book will help equip you for this. For those who go into this arena without the years of experience a seasoned marketer brings, the amount of time and effort needed for marketing your game can quickly add up—contributing to the already sizable amount of work you already have in front of you. There can be benefits to bringing others on board who can dedicate time and attention to marketing so your team can focus on development. If you delegate marketing to others, this book helps you address marketing topics intelligently and contribute in an informed way.

Options for Marketing Staffing, Beyond Yourself!

Add a marketing person to your team: You could begin with a part-time marketing person, particularly early on. Or you might have a member of your development team who can take on marketing responsibilities—a person who has time available to fit with their regular workload and appropriate core communication skills.

Establishing a general email account, such as "contact@studio_name.com", that multiple people can access (e.g., through webmail), can work well. It's important to establish continuity for communications. So if you have a person who can only assist with marketing on a part-time basis, others can jump in on a shared email account to keep conversations moving forward—with press, partners and other contacts. Nothing kills momentum or squashes potential opportunities more than gaps in communication and lack of responsiveness. Make sure this contact information is easy to find on your website—to help interested journalists get in touch with the appropriate people on your team.

> **Tip:** Be diligent! Lack of responsiveness and lags in communication can kill momentum and potential opportunities. Even a quick acknowledgement like "Got your voicemail" or "I'll get back to you on this later in the week" is better than no response or a reply that comes days or weeks late.

Hire outside specialist(s): You'll find many flavors and varieties of outside specialists—ranging from individual freelancers to mini agencies and larger firms. Some focus on PR, others specialize in advertising, and others offer cross-disciplinary product marketing expertise. If you're considering this route, talk to a few and determine what fits best for you—including your budget.

As You Grow

As your studio grows, you'll come to the point where you'll need to map out a longer-term strategy for your marketing staffing. Some opt for a medium-to-larger size agency, ideally with consistent people assigned to your account over time.

Alternately, adding a dedicated marketing person (or more) to your team can bring a number of advantages:

- Press and partners like to hear from the studio and speak directly with the team.

- A dedicated marketing person on your team can bring a higher level of attachment and connection to your mission and projects. They can work nimbly and adapt quickly to project changes as they happen.
- A marketing staffer can optimize access and communications. They can also gain insights and experiences with the project and its unique characteristics that they can share with others through their higher level of contact with the team and project.

Note that this book's author has worked as on-site staff, and that influences the perspective of this section.

Recommended Exercises:

1. Draft marketing fundamentals for a game.
   - Create these for a game you are considering for development, are currently creating or have launched in the past or even for a favorite game you've played.
2. Craft marketing messaging.
   - Write a positioning statement, elevator pitch and tagline.
   - Try your elevator pitch and/or tagline on friends, family, colleagues.
   - Make a quick mock-up with an image from your game combined with sample taglines.

Notes

1   Al Ries and Jack Trout, 1981. *Positioning: The Battle for Your Mind.* New York: McGraw Hill.
2   Adapted from Rosser Reeves, 1961. *Reality in Advertising.* New York: Knopf.

Chapter 3
Branding
Guest Author: Tom Byron

For indie game developers, branding can be just as important as it is to big publishers. Branding has broad implications, as it can form the very foundation of *everything* you and your company do, not just marketing, but strategy, hiring and company culture as you grow—and even how you distribute your game.

Some dismiss branding as peripheral, terminology from the realm of corporate marketers. You already know what you're all about—you just want a marketing plan, right?

Chapter Objectives:
- Articulating the role of branding, particularly as it relates to games.
- Providing building blocks for determining your brand.

You don't approach your game development casually, and the effort you put into your brand should be equally committed. It's true that some—many—brands arise naturally and unconsciously, either from the game or the personality of the game creators. This doesn't negate the need to establish your brand in a smart and comprehensive way.

So . . . what exactly is "branding"?

Branding: The Philosophical and the Practical

Branding can be broken down to two inextricably bound parts: the philosophical and the practical, in that order. Let's take a closer look:

The Philosophical

The philosophical side of branding includes defining your brand, establishing your studio and game "personality." It's finding the words that best describe your company and game. It's discovering the "who," the "what" and perhaps most significantly the *"why"* of you and your product—not just today, but well into the future. It includes your overall company strategies and affects every aspect of your business. Branding is your reputation. It's how people will talk about you, and it's how you *want* people to talk about you.

EA famously established the "If it's in the game, it's in the game" tagline for its Sports series. But this was far more than a slogan—it defined their sports games, it set expectations of the most realistic sports experiences on the market, and it did so for many years.

It's a promise that EA has had to keep, and their audience has held them to a high standard.

Which brings us to a favorite definition of brand: A brand is "a promise kept." Think about that for a moment.

The Practical

On a practical level, branding includes all the physical and administrative components of your company and game. This includes items like:

- Company and game name
- Company and game logos
- Messaging, slogans, taglines
- Advertising
- Website
- Trademarks
- Social media
- Marketing strategy and tactics

And so on. As we delve further into specifics in this chapter, you'll quickly see how philosophical branding logically and profoundly leads and guides practical branding.

Importantly, you should also view your games as part of your studio's practical branding. Each release plays a role in establishing the brand identity.

Brand Development

Your brand is *who you are* or who you want to be. It's your stake in the ground that establishes your company and game personality. Even more importantly, branding establishes *why* you do what you do. When you are clear on this, you'll know how to communicate your brand to the world. Well-articulated branding is kind of the Zen state of marketing: everything that follows becomes clear. It's enlightenment in a very real way.

> **Tip:** Articulating your brand position early can help tremendously in guiding and unifying your studio's work. Many of the best companies, with the most loyal customer followings, can attribute elements of their success to strong branding.

Examples of Established Branding

It's useful to talk about examples of great branding that have stood the test of time, that have truly "made a promise and kept it" and have rarely veered from what they established. Of course there are thousands of great examples, but let's go with an easy one: Apple. Very early, Apple established a brand foundation of "no clutter"—keep it simple, keep it accessible, keep it clear. This ties to the core identity of Apple products: intuitive and easy to use. The result: Through their product and marketing, Apple has largely kept that promise. Their computers, iTunes, phones, ad copy, packaging, company culture—almost everything—lives up to this brand promise.

Compare Apple's brand message to Microsoft's, which decided years ago that "more is more," that is, provide the customer with as much information as possible, and make sure they know what they are getting by being (over)communicative. We'll not turn this into a debate about which approach is better: Both companies have been quite successful. However, they illustrate how each company established their respective brands—the promise they intended to keep—and how that brand manifested itself over the years, influencing and explaining why each company took the paths they took.

Very early on, Google decided it would "Do No Evil." This is a powerful brand statement. Have they kept that promise?

Let's now take a look at brands closer to what you do: games. Pick any gaming company. What comes to mind? Can you define their brand? When you think about it, is your impression based on your personal opinion, or the brand the company defined over the years? Importantly, it can take years to build a brand, but only a few days to destroy it. The assumption in this book is that you want every game you create to be the best it can possibly be, that you are committed to creating games that people will love. You don't have the resources (yet) to do otherwise. But, it only takes one game that falls short of your "promise" to undermine all you've worked so hard to accomplish.

Nintendo has famously put a stake in the ground of simplicity and accessibility not too dissimilar from Apple. They want to be all about the game, and they want an experience that the most people can play—not just gamers, but parents, grandparents, young children—in a word, everyone.

Finally, imagine if EA Sports decided to make a medieval-based RPG. What kind of reaction would that head-scratching decision receive?

The Brand Development Process: 8 Steps

Developing your brand is a process, and it doesn't need to be complicated. It does, however, require focus. But once established—with the end result being your "brand bible" or core message document—with some tweaks over time, it should remain powerful and relevant through the life of your company and games.

The brand development process depends on you, your focus, the level of importance you place on it, and your time relative to creating your great games. Yes, companies can and do spend thousands if not millions on brand development. Some companies spend hundreds of thousands of dollars on logo development alone.

You don't need to do this at a small indie studio scale. Brand development need not cost you except your time.

In the spirit of keeping it simple, the brand development process can be broken down into eight essential steps. Keep in mind, these steps apply to both your company branding and your game branding.

1. The Facts

What are all the facts about your company or your game? The founders and their roles, where you're located, your background, expertise and really anything and everything that will establish the basic facts about you and your studio and game(s).

2. Answers to These Essential Questions

- WHY are you?

  We know what you're doing, but why are you doing it? What motivates you? What gets you up in the morning (or night), ready to tackle whatever needs to be done to accomplish your goals?

- What makes you special? If someone were to say "so what?" when you first mention your game or company, how would you answer?

- Why should people like you? Your company? Your game?

Approach these questions thoughtfully and objectively. Developers can get very close to their work or get jaded, and they need to step back and think about this—about elements that they may not initially think of as special, which others who aren't as familiar with their world might!

3. Create Your Brand "Personality"

Like anyone's personality, your company or product brand personality
is similar. How would you describe that personality? Here are some
example descriptive words and phrases to think about when developing
your brand personality:

Table 3.1 Sample Brand Personality Descriptors

Independent	Ambitious
High quality	Strategic
Great [with specific attribute(s)]	Bold
Funny	Risk-taking
Serious	Confident
Determined	Aggressive
Engaging	Accessible
Challenging	Dedicated
Best [with specific attribute(s)]	Committed
Expert	Craftsmanship
Inspiring	Thoughtful
Artistic	

Here you can also insert what YOU aspire to, as in "We're the next Zynga"
or "We're like EA when they first started" or "we want to be like Double Fine."

In this part of the brand development path, honesty is absolutely critical.
Remember, a brand is a promise kept. Don't make claims you can't defend
(that is, promises you can't keep). Don't say you're "the best," or your game
is "the best" at something if you can't prove it. However, you can say "we
aspire to be the best" or "our game does this one thing really well." Be bold,
yes! Be positive, yes! Be aggressive, yes! But above all, be honest, YES!

When articulating your brand identity, go for a unique and distinctive
position. If you're going for an aspirational position, strive for one that
you feel is achievable and not overly lofty.

> **Tip:** When articulating your brand personality, make sure you steer
> clear of generic terms or descriptors that could apply to any
> number of companies.

4. Competitive Landscape

Who are the current leaders in your field? What games out there are
closest to yours and who are the market leaders? Why do you believe
they have been so successful? Knowing what you're up against will only
make your company and game stronger. Look also for insights based on

companies and games that haven't performed well and the reasons why they haven't.

5. Target Audience

Significantly, your audience defines your product and marketing. Your audience is your customers, they are the ones who will purchase your game and buy into—and grow—your company's future games and vision, and yes, your brand promise.

> **Tip:** Think of your audience—both real and targeted—as the heart and soul of your company—win them and you *win*, believe in them and they'll believe in you. Respect them and they'll respect you (by purchasing and evangelizing your games).

So, who do you *want* as your customers? Who do you want to buy your game? Determining your players may be obvious and easy based on your game. If you're making a sci-fi based FPS, you're going after the *Halo* crowd. There's your primary audience: FPS gamers who love *Halo*.

But what if you're making a quirky and humorous RPG based on characters from *My Little Pony*? It's too easy to believe *My Little Pony* fans will love it just because it's based on their favorite show. You have to appeal to RPG players too.

You can get insights on your audience partially by gauging responses to your games, demos and marketing materials. Assess the kinds of people your game appeals to at shows and talk to them about what prompted them to check it out after they're done. Ask them what they liked and didn't like. This can help establish an even better definition of who your players are, and *why* they are. You may find yourself adapting your intended target audience assumptions based on these kinds of experiences. Don't try to brute force an audience you hope or believe should like your game.

A quick note: Your target audience is never "anyone who likes games" or something similarly obvious. This is a vague, dismissive and cynical way to approach your audience.

You Are the Company You Keep

Determining who you want your customers to be can help determine how you will interact and speak to them. It further determines to whom and how you'll speak with the press. Getting a story about you or your game in the *New York Times* sounds awesome, but if you're looking to reach hardcore gamers who are most likely to purchase your product, it would probably be more of a coup to get a piece on, say, IGN.

6. Differentiators

What makes your company or product special? How does it compare to other companies? What differentiates you from the thousands of companies and games out there? What are the one to three statements you can make that clearly answer the "so what" of your game?

7. Your Brand/Mission/Product Statement

It's time to write your brand statement, also known as the mission statement (or "pitch" statement). This is NOT a slogan or tagline. Rather, this is a statement, primarily for internal use only, that encompasses all that you are with one compact, efficient and clear articulation. Here's an example based on the earlier "brand trait" examples:

> *[My company] is committed to creating the most challenging and engaging RPGs today. Our expertise and dedication will ensure the highest quality, and our sense of humor in our company and games will remind us that we're all in this for the fun—and if we're having fun, our players will have fun.*

Once you've established this core statement, you'll need to commit it to memory. It will become the driving force of the company. You'll also practice saying it in different ways depending on the situation. Provided that your brand statement ties closely to core characteristics of your studio and team, memorization shouldn't be an issue. It should flow naturally.

Your core statement will likely have a long version, as well as a so-called "elevator pitch" version, because often you'll have less than a minute to make your point.

> **Tip:** Mount your brand statement on the wall in your office, install it as the desktop wallpaper on your workstation, make it your iPhone's lock screen. Keep it top of mind regularly!

8. *Your Brand Bible a.k.a. the Core Pitch*

Once you've determined all of the above, the result will be the Core Pitch (also known as your "brand bible"). This document will form the source of practically everything you do in marketing moving forward. Once established, your core pitch will be the inspirational and practical source for marketing strategy, logos, ad copy, tag lines, blogs, press releases, human resources, and presentations for funding.

The Practical Side of Branding
Naming, Trademarking, Logo Design

The practical or administrative side of branding is also largely the fun and creative part of the marketing process. Springing from all you have established in creating your brand, it's time to show what you've come up with in real-world ways.

As mentioned in the beginning of this chapter, all the assets you'll need for successfully marketing your game may come easier than you think. You likely have the raw talent available to you, either yourself or the person creating art for your game. Of course you can hire out the marketing-asset process depending on your budget—there are plenty of marketing consultants and designers out there, including some good work coming out of the plethora of inexpensive crowd-sourcing sites such as CrowdSPRING.com and 99designs.com.

A word on timing: In general, create marketing materials when you're ready—when you're ready to really talk about the game, within perhaps six to nine months of its release. When the press first write about your game, they will want screenshots at minimum, and a logo, character shots or designs at most. Of course, you can talk about the game well before this point, it's just that when it's time for previews—when you're close to release—don't be caught off guard when the media starts asking for assets.

With that, here's a basic checklist of the minimum base marketing assets every company or game should have:

- Company logo
- Game logo
- Screenshots

To take it a step further:

- Website
- Facebook page
- Twitter
- Core Pitch Presentation

Protecting Your Brand: The Legal Stuff

Because branding is outward and public communication about your company or game, it is vital that you protect your brand. After all, you don't want anyone to use your intellectual property—your game—inappropriately or illegally. Remember, this is *your* creation, *your* idea, and only you can/should dictate how your property is portrayed or sold.

The legal side of branding includes trademarking, such as the name of your game and your company. You do not have to hire a lawyer for this, at least not yet. You do need to make sure the name you came up with is not being used by anyone else, especially in games. A simple web search is a good place to begin.

> **Tip:** Once you've determined the name is safe to use, *start using it!* Secure the URL, create a website, talk about it in the press, and so on. The more you use it publicly, the more you will establish it as yours. This will help significantly in the trademarking process when you're ready and able to do that.

A Final Word on Branding

Branding is your identity, your professional DNA. It defines you. Yes, brands can and do happen organically and without conscious effort sometimes. But that is still branding! Branding happens whether you directly create it or not. In the end, it will be the level of control you take with your brand that can make the difference. Branding is important guidance for all: It helps to ensure a shared and articulated vision. If leadership is clear on branding and takes it seriously, then every single person you hire, every single person you work with—vendors, freelancers, etc.—should and will join in that vision.

Always being "on brand" is a beautiful thing.

Recommended Exercises:

1. What are core attributes for your studio (based on the studio as it is right now, or the desired position for your studio)?
2. Identify strong brands in gaming—large studios and small. Who's doing branding well and how? How can you learn from their brand building and carry that over to your studio?
3. Identify strong brands in categories outside of gaming—large organizations and small. Who's doing branding well and how? How can you learn from their brand building and carry that over to your studio?

Case Study: Klei Entertainment

Branding

Readers can see an example of a studio that's establishing a strong brand in Klei Entertainment, based in Vancouver, British Columbia.

For Klei, the studio's visual presentation provides a key unifying element across the company's different releases. While Klei's games vary considerably—from the colorful all ages *Eets* puzzler to the graphic side-scrolling *Shank* brawlers to the dark *Don't Starve* wilderness survival game to the stylish *Invisible, Inc.* tactical spy game—prospective consumers can quickly see that these all come from the same studio.

While the creative director clearly guides, unifies and defines the visual style, Klei builds out its brand by consistently delivering in a number of areas:

- **Richly expressed worlds**: Excellent presentation, attention to detail and nuance
- **Highly polished game production**: Strong craftsmanship through fluid animations, effects, controls and interactions
- **Focus on excellence**

One can see the Klei brand executions throughout the studio's work, including:

- **Game presentation:** Opening game screens, menus, interface and, of course, in-game content
- **Marketing materials:** Impactful key art with strong executions built around central characters; logo treatments that resonate and pop; game videos and cinematics
- **Company website**
- **Trade show booths**

The team also cultivates this brand through the connections it builds with the audience. Early access programs have played an important role in a number of releases, with responses to customer input by the team helping to guide the game's production. The studio has also built strong communications through social media, forums, trade shows and more.

Klei provides an excellent example of branding that isn't defined by a phrase, slogan or other verbiage. Without waving a snappy tagline in front of gamers' faces, the audience can clearly see the Klei brand shine through in the work the studio delivers. The brand unifies the games and influences the core game designs, production and delivery.

Concluding Notes

As with the world's most powerful organizations, the company and customers can benefit most in the end from effective brand building. When a game gains a strong following, customers become interested in other releases from the studio—both upcoming and back catalog. This opens up opportunities for cross-selling and merchandising programs periodically—and prompts loyal fans to spread their enthusiasm with their circle of friends.

Chapter 4
Developing Your Marketing Campaign and Calendar

Like game development, you should plan and schedule your marketing well in advance. This should include activities well past your game's launch date. Once you have the fundamentals from Chapter 2 in place, you can begin to create your plan—including marketing and sales goals, major marketing milestones, budgets, events and tactics.

> **Chapter Objective:**
> Learn how to create the marketing plan for your game—outlining key information to determine your plan development.

When to Begin Thinking about Marketing

Now! You should really begin thinking about marketing for your game at the same time you start development.

> **Tip:** Start thinking about marketing in the initial stages of game development. Your game and its ultimate success will benefit by factoring in marketing considerations early and often.

Create a powerful and effective plan for driving your game's success by starting your process with a few key assessments.

Determine Your Plan's Focus

Your marketing strategy and plan should first focus on these four points:

1. Target Audience: Who Are They? Who Do I Want Them to Be?

Identifying the expected audience for your game and assessing its viability will guide your game's development and marketing planning, and it should reap tremendous rewards for your project when the time comes to market it. Ask central questions about your desired customers: Are you making a game for non-gamers (such as *Solitaire*), casual gamers (a la *Angry Birds*), or hardcore gamers (*Call of Duty*)? Are you making a game for children or adults? RPGers or FPSers? Humorous or dead serious?

When asking these questions about your audience, you might find answers that change the way you approach your game design and goals.

Will you create a game for a broad audience that could generate large sales volumes or are you considering a game for a relatively small or oversaturated genre with smaller sales potential?

A market/audience evaluation early on can help guide you to projects with the greatest opportunities for success when release time hits.

> **Tip:** Define your game's target audience and key meaningful differentiators early on to help provide focus for your project. Post these prominently in your work area to keep them clearly in your sights!

2. Differentiators: How Will My Game Stand Out?

By thinking about possible unique and compelling characteristics for your game from the very beginning, you can make the process of marketing the game considerably easier. Identify possible hooks, such as a fun new approach to gameplay that's never been done before, a breakthrough mechanic that showcases a new hardware device or features, highly stylized visuals that will grab players, interesting central characters, storyline and setting, etc.

At the same time, determine hooks that your target audience will find meaningful and attractive. Avoid differentiators and unique features that won't grab players' interest. Consider informal or structured sessions (with friends, family, significant others, industry contacts) for getting feedback on your game concepts early on.

3. Launch Date: When Do I Plan to Release My Game?

Deciding your game's target release date can help to guide your marketing. Or, marketing ideas may influence your release date. For instance, if you're creating a game intended for kids, with a development schedule that will land on a springtime release, you can consider including Easter-themed content to add timely appeal and launch it on Easter week. Or if you're making a game inspired by the Olympics, then you'll want to let your game begin when "The Games Begin!" Puns aside, this illustrates one way that a marketing hook can help shape a launch strategy.

Alternatively, you might find yourself gravitating to one game concept on your whiteboard over another based on a seasonal theme. This may help to provide the kicker you need for an idea or spark thinking for new kinds of projects—perhaps a Valentine's Day challenge to play with a loved one, a Father's or Mother's Day game for sharing with a parent, etc. Seasonal content can provide excellent fodder for update releases and downloadable content to keep your game fresh and relevant and for post-launch marketing initiatives.

Think also in terms of less traditional holidays and events. "Talk Like a Pirate Day" is an example of a made-up celebration that generates interest every September 19. If you're not familiar with it, look it up, and you'll find that there's lots of fun pirate-themed chatter and interest around this date. Alternative approaches like these can work very well for marketing—sometimes better than crowded traditional holidays— such as the anniversary of a major event for guiding release plans for a related game concept. For example, a game based on World War I could release on the Treaty of Versailles's centennial anniversary.

Be wary: There's never a shortage of new Christmas-themed games every December!

4. Announce Date: When Should I Tell the World about the Game I'm Making?

Announcing your game (different from launching your game) depends to a degree on the nature of your studio, team and project. The announcement usually precedes the game launch. In formulating your announcement strategy, you will need to decide when and how you'll approach this and with what supporting content.

A first-time project from a relatively unknown set of developers, who don't come from higher profile studios or projects, might call for a different approach to the game announcement than a follow-up game from a larger well-known studio with an established audience and following.

> **Tip:** Key considerations to factor in when determining your game's announcement date:
> - Seasonality
> - Important developing news stories
> - Industry events

As you map out your announcement plan, be sure to look at key factors in the category. November and December, for example, can be challenging for announcing a new project because a large number of new game releases at this time of year tend to dominate the headlines, particularly very high-profile titles. Gamers and journalists focus largely on hot, newly available games during this season.

Factor big known seasonal sales into your plans as well. Launching your game just before, during or just after a big summer or holiday sale on Steam (or PlayStation/Xbox for console games) can put a big crimp in your launch momentum, and it's best to navigate around those windows. Communicate with channel contacts to get as much information from them as possible on big promo plans.

April Fool's Day, the internet's "favorite" practical joke day, would not work well for important announcements. Readers and press tend to write off communications on this day, generally not taking them seriously.

You should also look at industry shows. New announcements tend to cluster around notable events. A potential benefit to announcing at the time of a big event: media attention in connection with the show. At the same time, you might also be competing for coverage with numerous other announcements. For these reasons, consider breaking your news in the weeks prior to a show, so you can follow up with the media on site with additional information on your project. Media coverage opportunities can be lower after a show, because many journalists get overloaded with post-show follow-up and coverage commitments.

Monitor current events and major news while devising your announcement strategy as well, and be ready to revise your plans when needed to steer clear of stories that will come to dominate media coverage.

Consider *how* you'll announce the game as well. Can you tease it on social media, then unveil the reveal a few days later or at a big event? Can you arrange for an exclusive with a press outlet? Do you have the budget to work with PR professionals who have stronger press contacts than yours? Will you send out a press release?

Finally, determine your announcement support—beyond just letting people know that you're making a game. The more information you can provide to build interest as you get attention the better: game name/logo, brief description, genre, screenshots, concept art or video. The press appreciates and can leverage visuals for accompanying their articles.

Creating Your Marketing Roadmap

When mapping out the marketing timeline for your game, look at:

1. Creating Awareness, Sustaining Interest and Building to a Peak

The approach for establishing awareness and building interest can vary considerably from game to game and studio to studio. As mentioned earlier in this chapter, a new project announcement strategy from a popular developer will look considerably different from a first game announcement from a brand new studio.

Some projects take the approach of coming out of the gate strong at announcement time, going after a big splash—with a super-compelling video, a diverse set of polished screenshots, expansive game details and other impressive content—just a few months before the expected game release date.

For others, the game might opt to build interest over a period of time. Rather than spill the beans about the game all at once, they might plot out the timing for key information and content. For example, announce the game, release the first screenshots a few weeks later, then more information about the game, then a video. For this approach, devising an orchestrated schedule can help sustain interest in the game with the press and gamers so they'll continually want more and more until the game is available.

The chart below represents one kind of prelaunch through launch interest-building timeline. If you craft your plan with this approach, you can think about driving the shape of this curve and tactics that can help establish peak interest levels just as the game approaches its release window when people can buy.

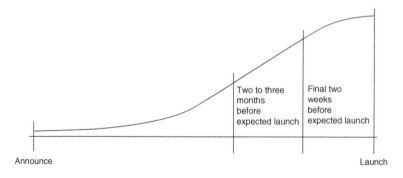

What is the best marketing timeline for your game? Some kick off their campaigns a year or more prior to their expected release date; others start just a few months before launch. A longer schedule can work well for a deeper game with greater breadth and scope.

Beginning too far in advance presents challenges in sustaining interest and enthusiasm over an extended period of time.

Ramping up too close to your release date runs the risk that the programs won't provide sufficient time for the game to register with your target audience and the press.

Some put out their first external communications only days before, or just as the game is releasing—and in some cases, after it launches. You'd likely run into challenges generating coverage for a game the press might perceive as old news. They tend to focus on the very latest and most topical information.

Try to build buffers into your schedule, as even the best laid plans can run into unforeseen bumps in the road and delays.

Whichever approach you take for your game, you can approach journalists in advance of the announcement date to seed the news and key assets. You can request that they hold off on posting them until your planned official announcement date.

2. Generating Interest and Momentum as Your Game's Release Date Approaches

To support your game's announcement and overall marketing timeline, think about the best content that you can build your plans around.

> **Tip:** Keep compelling content on reserve for sharing when you want your biggest interest peaks—just as the game is approaching its release date: impactful new videos, big announcements, reveals!

Examples of substantive content highlights you can build into your plan:

- **Big announcements/reveals.** Think about newsy announcements that can generate excitement—in-game content, new features, add-ons. You can also build interest and anticipation with the game's expected release date announcement. You may want to start with a season (Fall/Winter/Spring), before specifying the month or exact date (for example, "This game is expected to release Winter 20XX" vs. the much more specific January 15, 20XX). This approach also provides flexibility in case the date slips. Many will group the game's price announcement with the release date communication and might even open the game up for preorders at the same time.

- **Video.** These can be among the highest value assets you can share—showing your game in action. Be thoughtful in terms of how and when you share video content. To create effective video content, make sure to get your game visuals to a state that represents your intended look and feel.

  - You can use videos as the format for announcing your release date/price.
  - Your best asset might be a big new trailer, debuting just as the game launches.
  - Think about a series of trailers or engaging gameplay videos (focusing on different lead characters, themes, features), or sharing polished in-game cinematics prior to launch or "the first 5 minutes of the game."
  - Interviews, behind the scenes and live streams can also work well to capture interest.

- **Screenshots.** Prepare a plan for screenshot sets you can post periodically leading up to the game's release—showing as much variety as possible: different settings, characters, scenarios, a broad range.
- **Concept art.** While press and gamers tend to value in-game screenshots and videos most of all, concept art can be the next best thing. Concept art can work well particularly early on, before the game graphics are ready for capture. Even if concept art isn't part of your regular development plan, you might want to consider having some created for early marketing activities—to share the game's intended visual style around announcement time, to show the look and feel of different areas and to start generating fans.
- **Events.** Think about ways that you can coordinate with events in the months leading up to your release date. You may find it beneficial to look at this when scheduling key development milestones—so that they can align with notable regional shows, industry events, etc. In addition to getting your build in front of gamers by exhibiting at events, you can also pursue opportunities with press attending these shows.

- **Key Art / Hero Art**. For some games, the team can develop an iconic hero image to generate excitement. Think of this like the movie poster image or box art for your game. This kind of image might not necessarily make sense for every style of game. When it does, you can incorporate the key art into your asset reveal timeline.
- **Game code / review code.** At an appropriate time for your project, you'll reach the stage where you can share playable code with key influencers. This may be at an event, one-on-one visits with press or possibly builds you share with selected journalists. This can be a very effective way to pursue additional coverage, through preview articles and/or full game reviews.

Sources of Inspiration

Marketing campaigns from the world of movies and television can provide excellent sources of inspiration and insight for your project. Take a look at movie poster key art, engaging trailers, magazine ads, teases and the like. See how interesting franchises use social media, reveal casting and other announcements. You might get ideas from marketing programs in other categories too!

Chapter 8 provides an in-depth discussion of marketing asset Do's and Don'ts.

Recommended Exercises:

1. Create a first pass marketing plan draft for your next game based on steps provided in this chapter.
2. Document your observations for games that are launching right now. What approaches are they taking? Does this appear to be working well for them?
3. For strong performing games right now, which elements of their marketing plan appear to be working best for them? Can you come up with a reverse-engineered marketing plan outline based on campaign elements you observe?

Chapter 5
Marketing Vehicles That Can Work Well for Indies

As you'd expect, an indie game's marketing campaign will vary considerably from a large publisher's game launch. This chapter focuses on the kinds of marketing programs that many indies have used effectively, with relatively moderate budgets. AAA games, marketing campaigns can periodically provide inspiration and ideas for lower cost executions.

> **Chapter Objective:**
>
> Discussion of different kinds of vehicles for marketing games, focusing on those that can work best for indies at lower spending levels.

> **Tip:** Look for opportunities to market your game that:
> - **Get your game in front of relevant audiences.** Go after venues and programs for getting people to experience and play the game.
> - **Establish personal contacts and engage with influencers and gamers.** You'll find these personal contacts particularly beneficial as you continue building the presence for your studio and game. Cultivate relationships and gain supporters; these can yield returns as you grow.

PR

Given the power and potential for impact from press coverage, a separate chapter in this book dives into this topic in greater depth. Not surprisingly, journalists get many requests from game developers and publishers of all sizes to cover their games. Some games might not resonate for them as much as others. For this reason, you should establish marketing programs across multiple kinds of vehicles to supplement PR.

> **Tip:** While PR can work very well for indie games, it's not a silver bullet. Be sure to include other kinds of marketing vehicles and programs in your plans.

Audience Development—Social Media, Email and Beyond

Audience development merits its own chapter in this book for similar reasons, with the substantive gains these kinds of programs can help to deliver. In contrast to PR, you'll have direct contact with your audience through these activities and greater control and ownership of when and how you communicate, as well as your brand. You can benefit tremendously by establishing and building these channels as early as possible. This can become one of your best assets, driving the success of your game, subsequent releases and your studio. These kinds of programs can include:

- **Email**—build your list and establish a regular schedule of mailings to your subscribers
- **Community forums**—online and in-game
- **Social media channels**—Facebook, Twitter, etc. . . . and new vehicles as they emerge
- **Your website**—project updates, content posts (e.g., screenshots, videos), blogs, and more
- **Video**—YouTube channel and subscribers, live streams

> **Tip:** Start building your audience connections early—email mailing list, Twitter/Facebook followers, etc. You'll be thankful later that you started in the beginning and built your base continually over time as you get to a sizable audience and vehicles that you can use for communicating with them directly.

For best results, communicate regularly. For social media channels, you'll ideally want to post at least once per week. Communicating even more often can lead to higher levels of engagement and audience connections. You might start with fewer posts in the early stages of your project, and increase the frequency in the final months and weeks before the game launch when you have more content and news to share.

You can build affinity by posting on topics that do not connect directly with your project—comment on industry events, trends, other games of interest and more. That said, if your posts diverge too far from topics your audience finds relevant, you might risk losing some followers and interest.

Channel

Impactful channel marketing opportunities for indies can include feature slots at different store fronts, as well as periodic promo programs. Those who can establish relationships with representatives at those channels (Steam, PlayStation Store, Xbox Live, etc.) can improve their chances for securing these promo slots. Conferences and trade shows can provide an excellent setting for building connections, particularly at shows where these organizations have a booth presence. Stop by their space, introduce yourself, request business cards and build rapport with contacts. These teams frequently walk the floor as well. Keep an eye on the badges and company logo apparel of visitors to your booth and be sure to strike up conversations and collect contact information for notable people that stop by.

Events

Look for events where you can build visibility for your game, and explore different ways to establish your presence there. Along with valuable personal contacts and positive impressions you can create for your game at events, show organizers will often present additional kinds of marketing vehicles. For event participation, consider:

- Exhibiting your game on the show floor
- Submitting a proposal to speak on a panel or dedicated session at the event
- Purchasing space for promoting your game in signage around the event center and/or show guides
- Other marketing opportunities offered by event organizers

When event organizers present their marketing programs, they may include options with relatively low bang for the buck. Review and evaluate these with a skeptical eye.

Press and industry execs often attend events, particularly bigger shows in larger cities, and these can help in building your network. As suggested in the preceding Channel section, keep an eye on the badges and company logo apparel of visitors to your booth, and be sure to strike up conversations and collect contact info for press and industry people that might stop by your space.

> **Tip:** Look for ways to build your network of contacts through
> shows, events, meetups and more. These kinds of personal
> connections can yield tremendous benefits over time.

Promotions

You can set up periodic promotions to provide additional sales boosts
for your games. You can pursue inclusion in campaigns fielded by large
channels (e.g., holiday sales), and you might run other promos on your
own. While many focus on pricing promotions—particularly since these
can perform quite well—you can also arrange for different kinds of
initiatives. Look for ways you might add content or value in other ways,
rather than just slashing the price.

Examples of promotion types:

- **Time-limited price promotion.** These can span a single day, multiple days or a week (run rates tend to decline after one week).
- **Add on content.** You can expand your game's scope with new levels, characters, themes, etc., and establish promotional campaigns to help create exposure for this new content.
- **Holiday tie in.** Consider less common as well as traditional tie-ins for promotions, such as celebrating the beginning of summer/end of school year, start of spring, a presidential election, Friday the 13th . . . be imaginative!
- **Milestones**. Commemorate a game's initial release anniversary, "birthday" of a lead character in the game, unit sales peaks (XX,000 units sold!) and more.
- **Bundles**. Large established channels as well as dedicated bundle consolidators field bundle promos that have performed quite well with strong price and value propositions. Humble Bundle is one example of an organization that has generated sizable sales volumes for indie games.

Arrange for promotions several months after the game's initial release
to help in maximizing revenues early in the game's life cycle, as well as
initiatives at predetermined times later in the year.

Some will run introductory specials at launch time—particularly for lesser known games—to give prospective customers the final motivation they might need to make the purchase.

Awards / Competitions

Awards competitions can provide excellent ways to create visibility. You'll find relatively low entry fees for many of these. Awards evaluators—oftentimes, industry figures and influencers writing for popular websites or blogs—become familiar with your game through this process, which can lead to new opportunities.

Competitions often post finalists, providing more exposure. For those who win, the prizes and acclaim that come with victory help to open more doors for your game and generate additional visibility. Be sure to trumpet your achievements—including finalist selections—on your website, in your marketing materials, in signage at events, wherever you can!

Look for competitions of all sizes—large and small. Gamejams can also play a role here, with compelling game concepts and creators attracting interest through jam sessions.

Playable Code

Nothing shows off your project better than a playable version. While you can get your game in front of potential customers through appearances at regional shows, you'll reach the largest audience by distributing prerelease versions online: a public beta, demo or early access version of the game.

With a publicly distributed version, you'll want to make sure you don't include *too* much, so you whet the player's appetite for ultimately getting the final game!

You should generally schedule your playable public release for a date in relatively close proximity to your launch. Otherwise, the player's interest may wane or might get diverted to other games between the time of your playable code release and your launch.

> **Tip:** Don't include too much in a prerelease version of your game or post it too far in advance of your expected launch. Look for ways to use an early release to spark the audience's interest shortly before your game release approaches to whet their appetites for more!

Your Website

You have more control over your website than over most other vehicles. While many have created super flashy websites, with bells, whistles and fireworks, you should think about function over form.

Core elements to consider for your website:

- **Engaging central content** to draw viewers in and prompt interest in your game—such as a splash image or video
- **Timely news and project updates**, highlighted in a prominent place on your home page—perhaps in blog format
- **Prominent links for building engagement**—through your Facebook page, Twitter account, Twitch/YouTube channel
- **Email mailing list sign-up prompt**
- **Core game information**—game description, availability timing, platforms, how to buy, pricing
- **"About" and "Press" sections**
  - **About**—for more information about your studio, team, game(s)
  - **Press**—to assist press with covering your game, including contact info, key assets for download and possibly links to article highlights

Website stats tools can prove invaluable for tracking traffic as you ramp up your game launch, assessing how different initiatives increase visitors and interest at your site and assisting with evaluating program performance.

Paid

Through research and focused inquiries, you can find places to run paid ads that fit your budget best. You'll want to make sure you're placing ads with reputable organizations that reach a likely audience for your game. Smaller, focused outlets will probably work best for your budget, rather than large websites and publications which can cost quite a bit more.

This diagram visually maps benefits and challenges of different kinds of vehicles. While PR and channel programs can prove very impactful, marketers and game creators cannot directly control when and how they can get utilized. The channel and press gatekeepers are in charge there. You can control the message on your website, audience programs and public demos. Building out these areas can yield tremendous gains in reach and influence. While you can control the presentation and

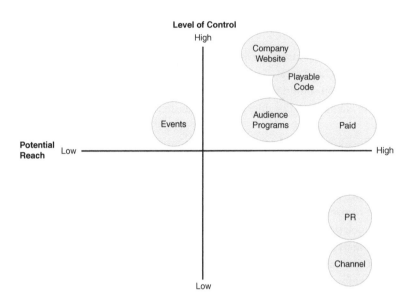

experience at shows, these reach a smaller audience at the event than other vehicles. Paid ad placements can reach a large audience, but you have less control over the communication environment.

Recommended Exercises:

1. Based on your game's characteristics, which vehicles do you think would work best for your next release and why?
2. Which indies do you think do a good job with each kind of vehicle described in this chapter? Document takeaways from this assessment to help with your next game marketing campaign.

Case Study: Supergiant Games

Preparation Meeting Opportunity

As discussed throughout this book, different teams have taken a variety of roads in the indie world. Supergiant Games, based in Northern California, provides an example that might seem like a dream from the outside. Taking a closer look, the team started from modest beginnings with many diligent days, weeks and months on development for its initial games and its own challenges. While they brought outstanding game development skills, instincts and inspiration to their projects, they also experienced the good fortune of very positive critical and gamer acclaim. As first-century Roman philosopher Seneca wisely stated, "Luck is what happens when preparation meets opportunity."

Numerous teams bring similar attributes to their projects and don't get to the same results that Supergiant achieved in its first years. Other case studies in this book show varying paths from different indies. Let's take a closer look at Supergiant Games, to see how this played out for them.

Amir Rao and Gavin Simon worked together at EA, and then formed Supergiant Games with colleagues that included other former team members and childhood friends. The leads had honed their abilities through a number of AAA projects, while cultivating ideas for their own games. When they took the plunge,

Supergiant worked out of Amir's father's house during the course of development for their first full game. Their team included Amir's childhood friend and *Dungeons & Dragons* group member Darren Korb, EA colleague and former videogame journalist Greg Kasavin and outstanding artist Jen Zee from the world of MMOs as well as comics and tabletop games, along with Supergiant chief technology officer (CTO) and programmer Andrew Wang and Darren's theatrically trained roommate Logan Cunningham to bring distinctive vocal character to the game.

As with other indies, Supergiant had a somewhat scrappy, ragtag, unconventional set up as it got started. The group's seasoning from earlier projects, creative inspiration, craftsmanship and love of games combined for something truly special in their first game *Bastion*. As described in the synopsis for the game on the Supergiant website—"*Bastion* is an action role-playing game set in a lush imaginative world, in which players must create and fight for civilization's last refuge as a mysterious narrator marks their every move." Supergiant developed the game with seven team members and contributors over a 20-month period, with its first release exclusively on the Xbox online channel.

After initial one-on-one sessions showing *Bastion* to friends and colleagues at the San Francisco Game Developer's Conference shortly after the studio's founding, Supergiant's first big break came when the Penny Arcade team chose *Bastion* as one of the esteemed PAX10. Not only did this selection provide validation and recognition for their hard work, it helped create a foundation for tremendous opportunities, which Supergiant capitalized on—visibility with consumers, press meetings, and more. Throughout these early days, the studio began executing a robust communications plan for audience development—with regular posts to its blog as an anchor. They also benefited from a multi-part behind-the-scenes video feature at Giant Bomb, which helped create a connection with emerging fans of the project and gave an inside look at the people and work involved in a project like this. While Supergiant may not have crafted an orchestrated plan for these initiatives in advance, they took advantage of opportunities as they came along with very positive results.

Fast forwarding: Supergiant continued ramping up activities around the game—in connection with the next year's Game

Developer's Conference and the Independent Games Festival, additional PAX events, E3, and more. Very high acclaim continued, with an excellent build to the *Bastion* launch on Xbox Live Arcade in Summer 2011.

At release time, top publications praised *Bastion*, and the game earned many awards and Best of Year honors including from *USA Today*, *Time*, NPR, CNN, *Wired*, *Entertainment Weekly*, Associated Press, Yahoo, IGN, and more.

Supergiant provides an example of a studio that has staged its releases for different platforms over time, with positive results. The team took the time to approach separate platforms thoughtfully, making the game the best it could be for each. They chose to have their internal team tune all versions, rather than outsourcing ports. The resulting reviews and game sales contribute to a validation of this approach for *Bastion*.

Within a relatively short period, Supergiant moved into production on its second game *Transistor*. *Transistor* carries forward a number of elements that characterized Supergiant's first game—Jen Zee's hand-painted visual style, the atmospheric narration and incredible craftsmanship, along with gameplay that reflects the team's many collective years as gaming enthusiasts and creators.

Concluding Notes

From modest beginnings in the living room of Amir Rao's father's home, Supergiant has achieved strong results for its initial games and positioned the studio well for future success. This came not only through early opportunities that the team capitalized on, but also many hours of diligent work, skill and very strong execution. It can be inspiring to see how well indie development and deployment can work when the stars align—while also looking at other indie stories where it might take two, three, four or more iterative game releases, with hits coming later on down the line.

Chapter 6
Developing the
Marketing Plan

Marketing plans vary considerably from one game to another.

As you might imagine, a movie studio wouldn't take the same approach to marketing a summer popcorn movie as it would to marketing a more literary boutique film.

When thinking about the best ways to market your project, start with a frank assessment of your game, whom it appeals to, and which kinds of marketing programs would fit best. While PR can often work very well, press interest might be lower for some games than others. Marketing plans for these games should include other kinds of vehicles—such as direct audience building and outreach, advertising and shows. The term "marketing mix" refers to the combination of different vehicles in the plan: PR, advertising, social media and so on.

Chapter Objective:

- How to approach your marketing timeline, channel and other specifics for your plan.

Tip: Develop a plan that balances different vehicles in the marketing mix. Don't rely exclusively on one kind of program—not just PR, promotions, etc.

The style of game, platform and audience will help to determine the marketing mix for your release. One would market a casual mobile game for young kids quite differently than they would a multiplayer death match PC game for serious players in their teens and older.

Paid, Earned and Owned Media

Some marketers divide marketing programs into three main categories: "earned," "paid" and "owned" media.

Table 6.1

Paid: Media you pay for	Examples: Banner you run on a website or ad network
Earned: Coverage you earn	Examples: Articles on websites about your game, word of mouth through Twitter/Facebook chatter, high view count for videos on your YouTube channel
Owned: Communication channels you own	Examples: Your website/blog, email mailing list, followers of your Twitter account, subscribers to your YouTube channel, fans of your Facebook page, participants in online forum you host at your website

Your marketing plan will determine how much attention you'll dedicate to which category of media and which fit best for your particular game.

When possible, create a plan where the programs support and complement each other: with paid media helping to drive growth for owned media, and earned media doing the same. Owned media can sometimes contribute to earned media, as when you attract press followers and other influencers to follow your social media accounts and/or join your mailing list.

> **Tip:** As you develop opportunities and traffic through earned and paid media, be sure to have your owned media optimized:
>
> • Engaging content posted on your website's home page can help in continuing to establish interest with new visitors attracted by your other programs.
> • Prominent messaging on your home page can prompt new visitors to sign up for your newsletter and social media so they can stay connected and informed.

Marketing Mix Throughout Launch, Build and Beyond

You will most likely emphasize some vehicles in the early stages of the plan and shift weight to others later on.

For example, you typically wouldn't invest money in ad banners until your game is available for converting traffic and interest to paid customers.

And while you can gain benefits from PR throughout your marketing campaign, it can fit particularly well at key stages like announcement time, the final weeks prior to launch and launch.

When all goes well, you will have built the size of your audience and owned channels leading up to the launch, and you can now alert these interested followers about the game's availability for purchase!

Sample Marketing Plan

Here's an example of a generalized roadmap, building backwards from the expected launch date [represented as "L" in this table].

Table 6.2

Timing	What	Tactics/Vehicles
L – 9 months (9 months prior to expected launch date)	Announce	PR/Press Release and/or through your website/blog/ social media if you'd previously built a reasonably sizable audience. Including assets like screenshots/videos/key art can make for an even stronger announcement.
L – 6 months	New assets reveal Concept art, screenshots, video	PR—article placements and/or through your website/blog/social media
L – 5 months	First playable code at industry/consumer event	Event Possibly supplement with PR
L – 4 months	Release new game assets— screenshots, character reveals, video Project update	PR—article placements and/or through your website/blog/social media
L – 3 months	Post first-look/teaser video and announce release timing	PR—article placements and/or through your website/blog/social media
L – 2 months	Project update	Blog post on your website and/or prompt for article through PR outreach
L – 1 month	Playable code to press outlets	PR—prompt for preview coverage, interviews
L – 3 weeks	Post new gameplay video	PR—article placements and/or through your website/blog/social media
L – 2 weeks	Distribute final review versions of game to press	PR—prompt for reviews to post at launch time
Launch week	Release launch trailer	PR/Press Release and/or through your website/blog/social media

Importantly, launch specifics should vary from game to game and you should not use the table above as a literal template for your own plan. Instead, look at this as an illustration of the points about:

- Building out a content plan and timeline leading up to your launch as described earlier in this book
- Using different kinds of vehicles at each stage leading up to release

Release Planning Across Multiple Platforms and Channels

Releasing your game simultaneously on multiple platforms and channels brings a number of advantages. With this approach, you can have the game available for as many prospective customers as possible at the same time—for people who play on different systems and gravitate to different purchase channels. Importantly, the interest and awareness you build through your primary marketing plan can then most efficiently support all of these versions. Alternatively, if you spaced out the release dates for different versions, you would need to rebuild interest and awareness each time out. This can be an important factor at the early stages of your project planning. Consider using multi-platform development tools like Unity.

Some have achieved success with staggered release dates across platforms. Your team may not have the resources to release multiple versions simultaneously. Or, you may take a judicious approach to development, in which you decide about secondary platforms after gauging the performance of your lead version. As you approach these decisions, you can factor in these marketing pros and cons. With staggered releases, you might also face perceptions of later releases as "ports"—with lesser attention and importance, after the fact. This can bring additional challenges in establishing interest with games press, partners and players.

If you can't get to simultaneous releases, you can go after target dates in reasonably close proximity to your lead platform launch to gain benefits from relatively recent awareness building.

Developing a Sustaining Plan

While a significant portion of your game sales will cluster around launch time, you can plot out programs for generating revenues afterwards as well. Marketing for your game shouldn't end when your game ships.

Specifics for post-launch programs will vary, depending on the kind of game you're creating. A later chapter covers this topic in greater detail. Post-launch programs can include:

- Add-on content and updates to generate new interest in the game—these can run the gamut from new features to add-on levels, characters, weapons, theme packs, etc.
- Community-driven contests, such as competitions, leaderboards, user generated content, fan art
- Planned post-launch price promotions and bundles

Tip: As with your launch, develop a calendar for the sustaining programs, scheduling out dates for new content releases, promotions, contests and more.

Schedule Recalibrations

Many continually adjust their development schedules as they go.

You should do a "reality check" on your schedule before you begin external communications and initiatives to determine feasibility of your desired release date.

Tip: Referring to an "expected release date" and a season will give you the most flexibility, e.g., "expected to release Spring of _____ [year]."

As your game gets closer to completion and the date solidifies, you might then want to refer to a release month—and then announce a specific date.

Contacts at key distribution channels should be involved in determining your final release date when possible, advising the amount of time needed to prep the game for release and optimal dates on their calendars.

Be sure to stay flexible. Schedule changes happen, and your marketing plans should stay open enough to evolve with them. The world will understand! Fans (most likely, including you) have seen many games revise their planned launch date before the final release.

You never get a second chance to make a first impression. You're better off recalibrating your schedule than sticking to an announced date and releasing a game before it's ready.

In the words of Nintendo legend Shigeru Miyamoto, "A delayed game is eventually good. A bad game is bad forever."

Recommended Exercise:

Create a first pass marketing plan for your game. You don't need to worry about creating a full, detailed plan document. You could even start with a rough outline and supporting bullet points.

Case Study: The Binary Mill's *Mini Motor Racing*

Marketing Plan Development—Launch and Beyond

For gaming companies of all sizes, plans too frequently fall into a common pattern—with most energies and efforts focusing on the launch window, to the exclusion of all else.

The Binary Mill's *Mini Motor Racing* provides an example of a game that mapped out scheduled post-launch programs, which have contributed to significant returns for the game.

Mini Motor Racing represented a different kind of game for the Australia-based studio: a brand new series for the company, not based on an existing franchise or licenses, in a new genre for the team—isometric arcade-style racer. The studio's past projects included a sci-fi shooter, apps partnering with Penny Arcade and Leisure Suit Larry's Al Lowe and a realistic gun sim. The team targeted *Mini Motor Racing* to launch on mobile platforms, where they'd gained traction with their past releases.

Mini Motor Racing integrated thoughtful game design for delivering a satisfying core game experience, along with in-app purchases for unlocks and upgrades—and for generating additional revenues.

This case study focuses primarily on the initial iOS launch platform—iPhone, iPod Touch, iPad.

The Binary Mill's launch and post-launch marketing programs included:

- **Launch Timing/Seasonal Content Tie-ins**

Mini Motor Racing planned for release in the active fourth-quarter period.

The Binary Mill team created fun seasonal content to help establish relevance, particularly in view of the competitive year-end launch timing.

- **Pricing**

The Binary Mill set an appropriate list price in comparison to competitive games, which also built in margin for later discounts:
$1.99 USD for iPhone version
$2.99 USD for iPad version

- **Promo Calendar**

1) The team scheduled *Mini Motor Racing*'s first price promo for three months post-launch:

$.99 USD for smartphone version (discounted from $1.99)
$1.99 USD for tablet version (discounted from $2.99)

2) A sizable 1.5 game update released six months after the initial launch.

The team expanded the magnitude of the update and marketing support—which had been initially conceived as lower level tuning—driving an additional sales bump.

3) A "Free App of the Day" promo came next on the calendar, seven months post-launch.

In-app purchasing helps to monetize the sizable volume increase.

4) Holiday Season #2

As the game's one year anniversary rolled around—and the winter holidays again—the team updated timely content from launch time. This included a seasonal update to the app icon, highlighting the holiday-themed track within the game, and a fun snow globe effect for the opening menu screen (swirling snow, tied to the device's accelerometer).

Updated icon for seasonal refresh at one year anniversary

Concluding Notes

As a brand new franchise for the studio, *Mini Motor Racing* performed well. The game drove millions of downloads within its first year across all platforms, and then extended into a full series, with follow-up *Mini Motor Racing* games.

After the iOS launch, *Mini Motor Racing* subsequently released on Android, PC/Mac, and even physical units in arcades!

Chapter 7
PR
Guest Author: Emily Morganti

PR (short for "public relations") focuses on managing how your product or company is presented to consumers. A lot of what you've already read in this book has to do with getting the message out about your game, so what exactly is PR when it comes to games?

In the game industry, PR mostly involves communicating with the press (writers for websites and magazines dedicated to games, people who cover games for consumer publications, bloggers, YouTubers, etc.) to make them aware of your game, so they can spread the word to their audiences. Press coverage lets your target audience know the game exists and, hopefully, convinces them to buy it. So for the purposes of marketing your indie game, PR is all about interacting with the press: how to find the people who will be interested in covering your game, how to approach them and what to say.

Chapter Objectives:

- Identifying ways to approach PR for raising visibility on your indie game.
- Discussion of different kinds of press, outreach and support materials.

Should I Hire Someone to Do My PR, or Do It Myself?

This chapter will give you a foundation for doing your own PR. Of course, there are firms and contractors who do this work all the time, who already have good press contacts that they talk to every day. If you don't have the time, motivation or skills to do your own PR, that expertise may be worth paying for.

Whether you do it yourself or hire someone, results are never guaranteed. If you hire someone to do PR for you, make sure you know what you're paying for and don't spend more than you can afford. Remember, you *can* do this work yourself. PR is crucial for spreading news about your game to the world, and lack of funds should never stand in the way.

Types of Press

When you reach out to the media with news about your indie game, categorizing publications can be helpful. Plan to tailor your message for different types of publications to make the game relevant to their audiences. Here are some categories of press that cover indie games:

- **Mainstream gaming press:** These are the top gaming sites and magazines, the ones you probably read yourself and dream of someday covering your game. As of this writing, some of the biggies are GameSpot, IGN, Polygon, Eurogamer, Kotaku, US Gamer, Destructoid . . . and the list goes on. There aren't as many print magazines as there used to be, but Future is one of the larger publishers still in the business, putting out magazines such as *PC Gamer, Games,*™ and *Edge.* Plus, most non-English-speaking countries have their own big gaming sites and magazines, many with staff who will cover games that aren't localized and don't mind corresponding with developers in English. Not surprisingly, mainstream gaming publications have big audiences, and their coverage can get your game great exposure among gamers. But it's also hard to get noticed by these types of publications—not impossible, but it takes work and a stroke of good luck.
- **Enthusiast gaming sites and blogs:** From smaller gaming sites to personal blogs, there are literally thousands of websites that cover games. Like you, the people who write for these sites are often indies themselves, writing for little or no pay because they love games and want to make a name for themselves in the industry. These sites may not get as much traffic as bigger sites, but getting coverage from them can still have good results, especially if you get a lot of sites covering your game at the same time. This sort of "critical mass" can even pique the interest of someone who writes for a bigger publication, who would have passed on the game otherwise.
- **Specialty gaming press:** Some sites specialize in a particular topic or genre that applies to your game. In the indie gaming sphere, this means sites devoted to covering indies, like IndieGames.com. For iPhone/iPad games, specialty sites include PocketGamer, Touch Arcade, 148 Apps, and Modojo. If your game is family friendly, seek out sites devoted to family entertainment and parenting advice. And for games in a particular genre, like adventure games or RPGs, sites like AdventureGamers.com and RPGFan.com should be high on your list.
- **Consumer / pop culture / tech sites:** Some publications cover games for a consumer audience (e.g., newspapers, magazines, TV

news), along with other media (e.g., movies/TV, music, comics), or under the umbrella of tech (e.g., gadgets, computer hardware, phones). These publications might be worth approaching with a slightly different message than the gaming sites, to highlight why your game is an especially good fit for their audience. Seek out editors and writers who have covered games in the past, rather than approaching the editor-in-chief.

- **Video streaming (e.g., YouTube, Twitch):** Video streaming sites have become popular channels for game coverage, although their "Let's Play" style videos are often different than typical game reviews. People who stream games are worth reaching out to, but maybe with a different approach than press in the other categories.
- **Freelancer writers:** Someone who writes for multiple publications, rather than being on staff with one particular outlet, is a freelancer. Get to know which freelancers like indie games or the type of game you're working on. When you find one who's interested in your game, they might be able to get articles in more than one place or secure coverage in a publication you weren't able to get on your own. But be aware that freelancers usually don't make editorial decisions, so even after you've found a freelancer who's interested in covering your game, they still have to find an outlet that wants to run the coverage (and might not be able to).

Types of Coverage

Here are the types of coverage you should try to get for your game:

- **Preview:** Coverage of a game that's not finished yet, usually based on information provided by your team, an in-person demo or the author's experience with an unfinished build (a "hands-on preview"). Previews are typically not scored and tend to be more forgiving than a review of the finished game.
- **Interview:** Q&A with a member of the development team conducted by email, phone/Skype, or in person. Interviews can be done at any point during a game's development, as well as after the game's release.
- **Review:** An assessment of the finished game, often with a score attached. This is the coverage you get at launch, and it boils down

to the press outlet recommending (or not) that their readers buy your game. All press is valuable, but reviews tend to be the biggest influencers on sales since they hit when the game is available to purchase. (So, someone who's convinced by a review that they want to buy the game can immediately do so, compared to reading a prelaunch preview and forgetting about it by the time it comes out.)

- **Feature:** A story about a specific angle relating to your game or your role in the game industry. This can be the hardest coverage to get, because you don't know when a publication is planning to do a story that's relevant to your game, so you can't offer yourself up to comment. But if you make yourself easy to contact and get to know people who write about games, hopefully they'll come to you in the right situation.

- **Guest article:** Some sites post guest articles or blogs written by developers. Gamasutra, for example, often publishes post-mortem articles where developers outline what went right and wrong with their game project. Sometimes a site will approach you for this type of piece, but more often you'll need to come up with an idea and approach them.

Building a Press List

When it comes to promoting your indie game, one of your most valuable assets is a good press list. Your press list should contain the names and contact details of sites you hope will cover your game, as well as individuals who write for those sites. Just like building a mailing list of consumers interested in your game is critical for spreading news to potential customers, building a press list that's relevant to your game is central to game PR. Generating this list takes some work and it's important to keep it up to date, but this work should pay off both for this game and any game you make in the future.

At some point, your game had just one line of code, and likewise your press list will start small—just a few names on a spreadsheet. If you've already had some press coverage, either for your upcoming game or previous work, start by adding those publications and authors to your list. Continue to build the list a little at a time throughout your game's development, so when you're ready to reach out to press you already have a head start.

> **Tip:** Many websites make contact info publicly available (look for
> the About Us or Contact Us links). If not, you can often find a
> writer's email address through a Google search. Or, reach out
> through social media like Twitter or LinkedIn and ask for an
> email address you can use to keep them up to date on new
> game news.

Should I Really Add People Without Asking First?

Asking first would definitely be the polite thing to do. But it takes more
work, and if someone doesn't write back that doesn't necessarily mean
they won't be interested in your news. (They just might not realize it
yet!) As long as any bulk emails you send have an Unsubscribe option
and conform to the CAN-SPAM law, don't feel bad about adding a publicly available email address to your press list. (But if someone does want
to unsubscribe, remove them—politely and promptly!)

How Do I Grow the List?

Look online for articles about games like yours and add their authors
to your list. As you identify games similar to yours, Metacritic and
GameRankings are good resources for finding reviews. Is there a site
you really want to see cover your game? Add it, either with the "catch-
all" email address (often something like tips@sitename.com or news@
sitename.com) or the most appropriate editor (some sites have different
editors for different platforms, a specific reviews editor, etc.). For sites
that only have a contact form, use this to ask for an email address you
can use for game announcements and news tips.

> **Tip:** Make a goal of adding 5–10 contacts to your list each week,
> and by launch you should have a good base of people to mail
> to. And remember to explore different categories—you want
> your list to have a good mix of press, so your news reaches
> different audiences.

The format of your press list doesn't have to be fancy; an Excel or
Google Doc spreadsheet or simple database will do. Give yourself a spot

to write notes so you'll remember why you added someone later or can keep track of discussions you've had with different journalists and publications. And categorize the sites so you can easily export a list of people for certain types of news. You don't necessarily have to use the same categories outlined above—whatever works for you. For example, if you're developing a multi-platform game, you might want to tag contacts by platform, so news about the mobile version doesn't go to PC-only press.

Other Ideas for Building Your Press List

- Gaming shows like PAX or IndieCade often provide a press list to developers exhibiting games there. For those that don't, ask the organizers if they'll give you the registered press list. They might say no, but it doesn't hurt to ask!
- Ask developer friends who have shipped games which sites and press contacts have worked out well for them. Maybe a friend can even make a personal introduction.
- Look online for lists of indie-friendly press contacts. Some developers maintain lists like this to help other indies.
- Assuming your website is hooked up to Google Analytics, keep an eye on your referrals. If you get a bump from a particular site, try to figure out where it came from and add the site to your list if appropriate. Sometimes a link gets posted in comments or on a forum, so even if the site itself didn't cover your game, the resulting traffic shows that their audience is interested.
- Make sure that your own website clearly posts the best email address that interested press can use to contact you. You may want to establish a separate press@ or pr@ email address to keep press requests separate from other correspondence.

How to Talk to Press

When promoting an indie game, you may communicate with press mostly through email. Keep your communications focused and to the point, but also talk like you're talking to another human being. Trying to be formal with your language, using a lot of buzzwords or being too cute in an attempt to grab someone's attention is a great way to be ignored. Many journalists appreciate that indies are *real*; talking directly with a developer can be a breath of fresh air from the hyper-controlled messaging they get from the PR departments of large gaming companies. This can work to your benefit.

Make it as easy as possible for the person you're emailing to cover your game. Besides being busy with their own work, these writers are constantly being poked by developers who want coverage. The easier you can make it for the press to cover your game, the better your chances of succeeding.

> **Tip:** A good subject line is critical—the press get tons of emails every day and don't open many of them, so make sure your subject line is specific and representative of what they'll see in the email. Job one: Get them to *open* and read the email!

Throughout your game's development, you'll be sending different types of emails to the press:

- **Introductions:** A "hi, nice to meet you" type email is a great way to make contact with someone you've noticed is interested in your game. When you see coverage of your game, drop a thank you note to the person who wrote it. Hopefully they'll remember the gesture when it comes time to cover the game in more depth, and now they have your email address so they can contact you if they want to. Alternatively, you can send thanks to a journalist or website over Twitter for covering your game.
- **Targeted preview / interview / review pitch:** A "pitch" is an email that suggests a certain type of coverage. Pitch the people/publications you want covering your game as you hit milestones in your development. For example, when you have a stable beta build that represents the game well, this would be a good time to pitch hands-on previews.
- **Big announcements:** Unveiling your game for the first time, setting the release date, posting a new trailer, putting out a demo, starting preorders, launch day—all of these events qualify for "big announcements" that you can distribute to your press list. Some of these are worthy of a formal press release, while others might warrant a detailed but less formal email.
- **Preview/review copy distribution:** You'll need to send this sort of email when you have a build ready for press to evaluate. It should include all the relevant details the previewer/reviewer needs to

know, such as where to download the build, any special installation instructions, known issues in the build, and the embargo date (when they should hold their coverage until).

- **Follow-up:** Whether it's a pitch to someone you really want to check out your game or a reviewer who never ended up posting a review, follow-up emails help keep things moving. Even with a good subject line, it's possible for emails to go into the spam folder or just be overlooked. Keep track of when you emailed someone (in a column on your press list spreadsheet, for example) and if you haven't heard anything a week or so later, send a follow-up. This doesn't have to be long; a quick "just making sure you got this" will often suffice. But don't put pressure on the person or make them feel bad for not writing back. If they've already decided they're not going to cover your game this time, repeated follow-up emails could make them reluctant to cover you in the future, too.

When organizing press communications, it can help to think of an upside-down pyramid as shown below, with the most important information at the top and less important details further down. When journalists have limited time and are just skimming their emails, this format helps them get the key facts before they move on to the next message in their inbox.

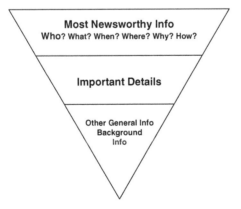

Also, make sure you're timely and responsive when working with press. Journalists frequently work on deadlines, and if they don't hear back from you in time, they might just move on to the next game on their list.

Adapt your communications for the kind of person you're reaching out to as well. For example, a writer at a hardcore gaming site probably thinks about games differently than a writer for an indie-focused site, and both of those journalists are likely more entrenched in games culture than a writer for a regional newspaper—even if you're saying basically the same thing to all three of these people, you should say it in different ways. YouTubers and streamers are generally most interested in getting review codes sent to them when the game's available, rather than advance pitches on new screenshots. When you tune your communications for the specific recipients (their favorite kinds of games, platforms they cover most, past articles they've posted, etc.), your chances of success increase.

That being said, even if you do a great job with your press communications, you won't get all the coverage you want, all the time. Sometimes a journalist's subjective taste, or the taste of the editor they're writing for, means a certain story can't find a home in a certain publication. Other times, even if everyone involved is eager to make the coverage happen, time or space constraints can get in the way. Try not to get discouraged. Learn from your experiences, and just keep at it. Trying, trying and trying again is the best way to go after press coverage in the long run.

Throwing a Good Pitch

A good pitch letter should be brief (no more than 4–5 short paragraphs) and clearly state why you're writing to the person and what you hope to result from the communication. When possible, you should personalize the letter to make it relevant to the person you're sending it to. One easy way to do this is to state in the first line that you saw their coverage of Game X and think they'll also be interested in your upcoming Game Y, for these specific reasons.

Sample Pitch: *Octagon*

Octagon is an arcade game inspired by the indie hits *Super Hexagon* and *Boson-X*, which released for Mac and iPhone/iPad soon after Apple rolled out iOS 7. Here's the pitch letter that went out to potential reviewers:

Subject: *Tron* meets iOS 7 in "*Octagon*", new arcade game out Nov 7—want iOS/Mac review copy?
Dear [name],
Imagine if the movie *Tron* had been set within the iOS 7 interface. That's what you'll get with *Octagon*, a minimal arcade game coming to

iOS and Mac on November 7. *Octagon* is a cousin to recent hits *Super Hexagon* and *Boson-X*: fast paced, intensely challenging, and unexpectedly beautiful with its colorful yet minimalist graphics. Can we interest you in a review copy?

In *Octagon*, you're trapped inside an 8-sided tunnel that never stops moving. Your goal is to survive each 60-second level without falling out. (It would be pretty simple if not for all the speed bumps and gaps in the way . . .) Flick the screen horizontally to spin the tunnel, flick vertically to flip upside down, and most importantly don't stop to think—*Octagon* moves too fast for that! Only super-quick reflexes will get you to the finish line.

Octagon has unlimited, procedurally generated levels, a trippy visual style influenced by the minimalist iOS 7 aesthetic, and music by electronica artist Sqeepo that keeps the adrenaline pumping. Upon its November 7 release it will sell for $1.99 USD or equivalent, with no in-app purchases to water down the challenge.

You can get an idea of *Octagon*'s look and feel from this gameplay video: https://everyplay.com/videos/1086351

Screenshots and a press kit are available at the official website: http://octagongame.com

We hope you'll check it out for yourself:

- iOS App Store: [promo code provided]
- Mac App Store: [promo code provided]

If you decide to review the game, we ask that you hold your coverage until 8:00 pm Eastern time on November 6.

Thanks!

— Petr Fodor and Lukas Korba, developers
Octagon press pitch used courtesy of Lukas Korba and Flow Studio

In this example, the intriguing subject line—which includes an interesting premise description, platform and release date—encourages the recipient to open the email. A question mark can help in an email subject line because it prompts the reader to take action with a reply.

The first paragraph distills the most important information about *Octagon* and ends with the reason for writing (an offer of a review copy). The reader knows right away that continuing to read the email will yield more information about a game they're being asked to consider for review. This particular email proactively provides a review code, rather than asking the recipient if they'd like one, cutting a step out of the process and making it easy for the journalist. If codes are limited or you want to keep close tabs on which journalists are considering coverage, you might instead want them to write back to request a code. Or you can try different approaches for different types of press (for example, provide a code for harder-to-get consumer and big gaming press, to make things as easy as possible, but ask people from smaller gaming sites to write back and ask so you can keep better track of who's interested).

The pitch email's second paragraph dives into the gameplay, describing the course (an 8-sided tunnel), the levels, the controls, the fast pace, and that quick reflexes are required. The developers wanted to attract people who like very challenging games, so they emphasized *Octagon*'s difficulty.

Next the pitch states the most important features, the price, and the absence of in-app purchases (which the developers noticed consumers and press had been complaining about in similar games).

Finally the developers provided links to assets (trailer and screenshots), access to the review copy and an embargo notice. While this pitch exceeds five paragraphs, the ones near the end are very short and the full email doesn't look overwhelming on the screen. Bulleting out key points and using bold headings are other ways to make your email easy to read.

You can see additional press communication samples in the supplemental section after this chapter—another pitch example and more.

This pitch resulted in launch week reviews from AppSpy, AppAdvice, Cult of Mac, *PC Magazine*'s AppScout column, Arcade Sushi and iMore, among others. The game was also featured in the App Store—something the developers had discussed with Apple separately, but good press always helps! A year after launch *Octagon* was still generating around $200/day, making it one of the developers' most successful titles to date.

Making Big Announcements

When you're promoting a game, not all news is big news. If you're just putting out a few screenshots or have posted a new developer diary on your blog, publicizing the news on your Twitter feed might make more sense than emailing your entire press list. The press get hundreds of unsolicited emails each day, and they're not going to read all of them.

But they will remember which names show up in their inbox again and again and again—not necessarily in a good way!

Save big announcements for major milestones like revealing your game for the first time, announcing the release date, and launching the game. Include all the details in your announcement that you're hoping to see in a news story. You don't want them to have to look very far to find everything they need to cover the news.

> **Tip:** For big announcements, give the press something meaty to write about, along with compelling visual assets like new screenshots or a trailer that they can include in their stories.

Traditionally, "big news" is announced with a formal press release that uses a lot of big, important-sounding language. For indie games, though, a less formal email (sometimes called a "media alert") can work well instead. Like the novelty of speaking directly to the developer, informal (but still well-written and informative) emails can be a nice change of pace from the stiff corporate communications journalists often receive from large publishers.

Sample Media Alert: *Cognition*

Cognition: An Erica Reed Thriller is a four-episode adventure game developed by Phoenix Online Studios. This game was announced with a Kickstarter campaign about a year before the first episode released, and the team did some PR during development, but when the first episode released it didn't get as much coverage as the developers expected. The following media alert was sent to gaming press a few weeks after the first episode's release in an effort to get more reviews.

Subject: *Cognition* (episodic adventure game from Phoenix Online and Jane Jensen)—want a review copy?

A string of grisly murders is going down in Boston, and FBI agent Erica Reed is taking it personally—her younger brother, Scott, was murdered by a serial killer three years ago. She also has an unusual skill at her disposal: a set of post-cognitive abilities that help her sense how a crime unfolded. As the body count builds, so does Erica's fierce desire to avenge Scott's death. The result is an engrossing point-and-click mystery that you (and your readers) won't want to miss.

Cognition: An Erica Reed Thriller is a four-part adventure series that recently debuted for PC and Mac with Episode 1: The Hangman. Review copies are available, and I'd love to hook you up so you can check out this tense psychological thriller firsthand!

If this is the first you're hearing about *Cognition*, here's a quick rundown:

- **A dedicated indie team:** *Cognition* is developed by lifelong adventure fans Phoenix Online Studios, the same guys behind the ambitious *King's Quest* spinoff *The Silver Lining* (which was praised by *KQ* creator Roberta Williams herself!).
- **Strong storytelling:** The "CSI meets Dexter" storyline was crafted with help from legendary designer Jane Jensen, whose portfolio includes *Gabriel Knight*, *Gray Matter*, and *King's Quest VI*.
- **Gorgeous graphics:** *Cognition*'s bold graphic novel artwork was overseen by artist Romano Molenaar, whose comic credits include *X-Men*, *Witchblade*, *Tomb Raider*, and many others.
- **Kickstarted before it was cool:** Months before Tim Schafer kicked off the crowd-funding revolution, the devs raised $35K on Kickstarter to begin *Cognition*'s development. Phoenix later teamed up with publisher Reverb Games to get the project completed and distributed.
- **Going Greenlight:** Thanks to amazing fan support, *Cognition* is ranked within the Top 100 games on Steam Greenlight (http://steamcommunity.com/sharedfiles/filedetails/?id=92915746). And it's already available for purchase from Rain, GamersGate, Gamestop.com, Green Man Gaming, and GameFly.

You'll find more info about *Cognition* (including a chilling trailer and some gorgeous screenshots) at the official website: http://www.postudios.com/cognition

Please let me know if you'd like to review *Cognition* for PC or Mac, and I can get you the first episode right away. (Ep. 2 will release soon after the holidays, so now's a great time to dive in!) There are also plenty of interview opportunities to go around, so if you want to cover *Cognition* but an episode review isn't the best fit, let me know and we can work out another angle.

Thanks, I hope to hear from you. Happy gaming!

— Emily Morganti
PR Consultant on behalf of Phoenix Online Studios
Cognition media alert used courtesy of Phoenix Online Studios

This email is on the long side, but it has a lot of ground to cover. The first two paragraphs summarize the game and explain why the email has been sent (episode 1 just released and review copies are available).

Then the email lays out five points that make the game unique—in a bulleted list with bold headings, for easy reading—to give context and convince people on the fence about reviewing that it's worth checking out. This particular mailing was meant to pique the interest of people who had ignored the game's release, so laying out these varied selling points was an important part of the message.

Finally, the email provides a link to the official website for assets and more details, as well as a recap of coverage opportunities available for press who write back.

This media alert resulted in about 100 review copy requests within the first 24 hours. Three weeks after the mailing, 50 new reviews had been posted online—no small feat considering this was during the Christmas/New Year holidays! By the time the *Cognition* Episode 2 review copy was ready, about a month after the initial mailing, the team had built up a list of 220 interested reviewers which kept growing as the 4-episode "season" continued.

Of course, the response your mailing gets will depend on how many people you send it to; the *Cognition* media alert went out to a few thousand. That's one way building up your press list over time can pay off.

The section following this chapter provides an example of a formal press release for a game announcement.

Tips for big announcements:

- Whatever format you use for your announcement, always present information clearly with the most important details near the top of the email.
- Include prominent links to assets and store pages you want the press to have access to. Keep these organized and easy to navigate—a massive zip file that contains every asset you've ever released is not recommended! You can link to a press kit page, host files on ftp or your own website, use a cloud-based drive like Dropbox or Google Drive or come up with another alternative that's easy and convenient for press.

- Like with a pitch email, the subject line for a big announcement should summarize the important details so the recipient has an idea of what they're going to see if they open it. Remember your subject line's top mission: Get the recipient to open the email!
- Don't assume the reader already knows about your game. Always give the genre, platforms, a brief description, and a link to more info (e.g., official website, press kit).
- Don't send attachments. If you want to include a few graphics, embed these with html rather than attaching them (but make sure they're not pushing your most important text too far down on the screen).
- Consider using a press release service for distribution: PRWeb, PRMac (for iOS and Mac news), eReleases and other sites can distribute your press release for a fee. If you haven't built a list on your own, a press release service is definitely better than nothing, but it won't be as targeted as the list you put together yourself. You could also do both—send it yourself and use a service—to cover your bases.
- No matter how you distribute your press release, always send it to GamesPress (inbox@gamespress.com), a free site that aggregates news for the gaming press.

Posting a Press Assets Page or "Press Kit"

Eye-catching game assets like screenshots, trailers, gameplay video and concept art can help press tremendously as they put together coverage of your game. The easier you make it for press to find and download compelling assets, the more likely they are to include these in their stories.

Your website should have a dedicated PR page, linked from the site's main menu or footer, that collects all of the game assets you've released throughout development. Organize and label the assets by date so it's easy to tell which are the most recent. You can link to this page in your emails so the press know exactly where to find the assets they need. Also make sure this page clearly provides information on whom the press can contact for more information about the game.

Check out http://dopresskit.com/ for a handy press kit template.

When to Talk With Press

Releasing a game without any press is like a tree falling in the forest with nobody around to hear it. Because of this, the single most important period for PR is the weeks just before and after your launch.

But is that enough? It really depends on the type of game you're making, your reputation as a developer and the resources you can devote to PR:

- Some indies like to announce a game early and tease it throughout development with videos and blog posts. This strategy can work well if you're already known in the industry and have a following among gamers.
- If you don't already have a following, announcing early might lead you to put a lot of work into content not many people will pay attention to. In this situation it might make more sense to stay quiet until closer to the game's completion and reveal it with a big splash and impactful assets when you can confidently give a release timeframe and details about which platforms the game will launch on, how the final version will look and play, etc.
- If you're pursuing Kickstarter, Steam Greenlight, or an early access release, you'll need to factor these sorts of activities into your PR plans.
- If you're planning to attend shows like PAX or GDC or to submit your game to competitions like the Independent Games Festival or IndieCade, the dates of those events should figure into your schedule in some way.

To maximize your efforts, come up with a schedule that makes sense for your game's development cycle and takes advantage of natural opportunities to share what you're working on. As far as announcing your release date goes—even if you're just announcing a general timeframe or a *year*—make sure you have a high confidence level in your ability to hit that date before you announce it. Missing a release date makes you look bad, and if this happens more than once, the press you're approaching for coverage (not to mention your potential customers) might start to feel jerked around.

There are four basic phases of PR activities that line up nicely with the stages of a game's development:

- **Way before launch (alpha):** Your game exists in a rough form, but it's nowhere close to being in a state where you want the press playing it or maybe even *seeing* it. If you have good reasons to announce the game this early (e.g., your fans are eager to know what you're working on; you'll be at a show where you can meet with press in person; you want to launch a Steam Greenlight or Kickstarter campaign), make this a "big announcement" with accompanying assets to pique interest and ensure the press will have meaty details to include in news posts.

- Even if you're not ready for previews yet, press may be interested in interviewing you at this point. If you do have opportunities to show the game to press, consider doing in-person demos rather than sending out a build, so you can cherry pick what you show and explain what's missing or how features that don't work yet will appear in the finished game.

- **A few months before launch (beta):** You're well into development now, with a release candidate on the horizon. If you haven't announced your game yet, now is the time. Some developers may choose to post an Early Access version, and can incorporate this into their communications strategy. At this point you might want to announce a release timeframe—not a specific date yet, but using wording like "early next year," "Q3," or "this summer," so press and potential customers have an idea of when to expect the launch.

  - A few months before your expected launch date, when you have a stable beta build with all features implemented and not much left to do besides polish and bug fixes, can be a good time to go after preview coverage. At this point you could let the press know that review copies will be ready in a certain timeframe and start keeping a list of people who are interested in reviewing the game.

- **Just before launch (release candidate):** Congratulations, your game is finished! But just because it's done today doesn't mean you should release it tomorrow. From the day your game is done, add another 2–4 weeks to the schedule so reviewers can play it in advance of launch. You can even give yourself longer if you need more time to find interested reviewers.

  - At this point you should announce the release date, if you haven't already. Make sure to discuss timing with channel partners before announcing the date, in case they want to change it. For channels that have a submission process (like the iTunes App Store or the Nintendo eShop), wait for your game to be approved before you announce the final date, just in case you have to resubmit.

- **Launch / post-launch:** On launch day, announce to the world that the game is available. Keep track of press coverage and update your press list so you can continue to use it for future PR efforts. In the weeks after launch, follow up with the reviewers who got advance copies and continue to distribute review copies to people who request them or new people you identify as good prospects.

As favorable reviews come online, you can incorporate these into your communications to continue building momentum—post good review quotes and scores on your online store pages, link to reviews from your blog or Facebook, retweet, the works. You can also include quotes and scores in ads, videos and other marketing materials, but it's good form to contact the journalist or publication's editor first to ask them if it's okay to use their quote in this context. Most appreciate this additional visibility for their byline, site or magazine. This also provides an excuse for you to contact the press so you can continue to build the relationship through friendly, courteous outreach.

Other chapters in this book talk more about timeline considerations for your press communications planning.

Distributing Review Copies

To give reviewers the best possible experience with your game, you should be prepared to send out a *complete, bug-free* review copy around 2–4 weeks before launch. When you distribute the review copy, make sure to include:

- A URL to download a standalone build or a redeem key if the download is through a channel like Steam or the iTunes App Store. You might want to password protect the download or add a "Review copy—not for public distribution" type splash screen to discourage piracy. Otherwise, the review copy should be exactly what consumers will get at launch, with an installer, all game features and few to no bugs.

- Important details that reviewers should know, such as where the game will be available, price, platforms and where they can download assets.
- An embargo date and time (with time zone). This is when reviewers can first post their review, and it typically coincides with the game's launch. Setting an embargo helps focus coverage on/after the day your game is available for sale, so people who read reviews can go buy the game while it's fresh in their minds. This benefits press as well, giving them a date to work toward and time to prepare coverage without having to worry about getting "scooped." Embargos also prevent bad reviews from hitting in advance and being the only recent coverage of your game in the days/weeks leading up to launch—this is no fun if it happens to you!

Keep in mind that an embargo is a gentleman's agreement, where you're asking them to accommodate your timing request in exchange for advance review code. Most press will honor it, but sometimes a review does go up early. If this happens, you may feel the need to contact the site and ask them to repost the review after the embargo lifts. Be polite—framing the wording in a friendly way, such as "We ask that sites post reviews after 10:00 am PST on May 1, 20XX, which is when we expect the game to release."

Rudely worded demands that sites take down a review or accusing journalists of ignoring the embargo could hurt your relationship with that writer or outlet in the future.

Tips for review copies:

- **Be generous.** As long as you have tons of redeem codes, don't be stingy. The more review copies you get out to people who will potentially write about your game, the better chances you have of getting coverage. You'll probably get more requests from small sites than big ones. As long as someone can point to a website, YouTube channel, etc.,

where they have covered games in the past and you're able
to verify that they're the same person (e.g., by matching
their email address to the address listed in on blog's contact
page), there's no harm in sending them a code and holding
on to their contact info. Even if their coverage doesn't yield
huge exposure this time, you never know which blogger will
be writing for a site like IGN by the time your next game
releases.

- **Beware of imposters.** Unfortunately, not everyone who
  contacts you for a review copy is above board. It's not
  unusual for people to write in claiming that they write for
  a big site or magazine, but are just scamming you for a free
  code. If the email address doesn't have the same domain as
  the website they write for and you can't verify their identity
  another way, you can ask them to write back from an official
  address or have an editor do so. It's not a big deal if you send
  a copy to someone who isn't legit, but that's not someone
  you want to keep on your press list for future announcements and outreach.
- **Never pay for coverage.** After you release your game, you
  might get a bunch of emails from websites offering to review
  your game for a fee. They make it sound like this is industry
  practice. It's not! Not only is asking for money in exchange
  for editorial coverage ethically shady, the exposure you'd get
  from that type of site isn't worth the money they're asking.
  If you're having trouble getting coverage, paying for a review
  might be tempting, but it's just going to make you poorer in
  the long run. If you do have money to spend on promotion,
  look into advertising or other paid marketing opportunities
  as described in Chapter 5.

How Can I Get Good Reviews of My Game?

Make a good game. Seriously. Games that get good reviews are the ones
reviewers had fun playing—games with a creative premise, good production values, clever gameplay and few to no bugs. The most obvious
way to get good reviews is by making a game that deserves them.

Tips for helping reviewers have a good experience with your game:

- Send out review copies well in advance, so they won't feel rushed to play it and finish the review in time for launch.
- Make a walkthrough or cheats available. Although reviewers usually want to experience the game exactly as a customer will, they also want to see the big picture, and giving them easy ways to experience "locked" content can help with this. If an aspect of the game isn't obvious in the advance review copy (such as in-app purchases that don't switch on until launch), find a way to simulate the experience for reviewers or at least explain how it will work.
- Be available. If a reviewer contacts you to say they've hit a bug or are stuck in the game, respond promptly and be friendly and helpful. "You're playing it wrong" type of responses usually don't go over well.
- When you see things you disagree with in reviews (which you inevitably will), don't argue publicly in the comments or even privately with the reviewer. This makes you look bad and might impact the type of press coverage your games get in the future. Occasionally a review is factually inaccurate and it's worth politely asking for a correction, but when it comes to a reviewer's opinion on the game's quality, entertainment value or anything else related to *their experience* (the whole purpose of a review!), just let it go. Try to learn from the feedback or chalk it up to someone who "didn't get it"—but keep that opinion to yourself!

Don't Give Up!

The strategies outlined in this chapter are recommendations, not rules—and there are no guarantees. When it comes to game PR, results are rarely instantaneous, and some relationships with journalists will have to develop for months or even years before they really pay off for you. Even if you're not seeing coverage right away, it's still better to put effort into PR than not. The more you reach out, the more you'll establish yourself among the press and the better your results will be in the long run.

So don't get discouraged if your efforts don't result in a flood of coverage the first time out. (Or the second, or the third . . .) Try to learn from your experiences. Even if something doesn't go quite right this time around, you'll have a better idea next time of how to do it. And remember that everything you're doing now isn't only in support of this game, but also of the hopefully many games that will come after it.

Recommended Exercises:

1. Identify key outlets for pitching your game and, ideally, specific contacts at these outlets.
2. Develop the basic pitch points for your game and ways that you would customize this for different press targets.
3. Create sample press materials for your game. If you already have press materials, evaluate them in the context of suggestions from this chapter and consider modifications.

Case Study: Additional PR Examples

Guest Author: Emily Morganti

To expand on ideas from this chapter, here are three additional examples of press communications, along with results.

Press Release

A press release is a formal way to announce your news, with a standardized format. These are best used sparingly, for your very biggest announcements.

Here's the press release that first announced The Game Bakers' mobile brawler, *Combo Crew*.

The Game Bakers' Combo Crew *Comes Out Swinging on iPhone, iPad, and Android This Spring*

From the makers of SQUIDS: *A modern, old-school brawler with platform agnostic co-op play*

MONTPELLIER, France—March 6, 2013—Mobile gamers, the fight is on! Indie developers The Game Bakers are revealing their next game: *Combo Crew*, a pocket-sized beat 'em up that combines innovative touch gameplay with good old-fashioned brawling. This action-packed game from the team behind the critically acclaimed SQUIDS and SQUIDS Wild West will release simultaneously for iOS and Android devices this spring.

In *Combo Crew*, a trio of heroes face off against hordes of enemies to fight their way to the top of the tower where they're being held hostage. When one hero falls, another can take over to climb the floors and advance the crew toward freedom. Inspired by the best of the arcade-era brawlers, *Combo Crew* puts a modern spin on classic beat 'em up gameplay with quick play sessions, solo and co-op game modes, a tower level structure, and an endless mode. And it's the first mobile brawler with cross-platform, asynchronous gameplay, so friends can rescue and revive each other from KO no matter what device they're using.

"With *Combo Crew*, we wanted to bring back the spirit of the old console beat 'em ups—the ones you used to play on the couch with your buddies—in a way that makes sense on modern mobile platforms," says Emeric Thoa, The Game Bakers' creative director. "Games like Street Fighter and Final Fight require a D-pad controller, and that just doesn't make sense for touch devices. So we challenged ourselves to make a brawler with really good touch controls. And we're pretty sure we've pulled it off!"

Combo Crew's intuitive interface combines highly responsive controls with exciting, tactile gameplay: swipe to attack, tap to counter, and use a two-finger swipe to unleash combo streaks unique to your character's martial arts skills. When your super combo meter is full you can trigger special moves, racking up massive high scores in the process! See how it all works in the first gameplay video: http://youtu.be/-20DW6gTK6E

Upon its release, *Combo Crew* will be available for download from the App Store and Google Play. Leading up to launch day, more details will be revealed at http://www.facebook.com/ComboCrew and @TheGameBakers.

About The Game Bakers

The Game Bakers is an independent video game studio based in Lyon and Montpellier, France. Founded and staffed by industry veterans whose credits include numerous AAA console games, The Game Bakers focuses on creative projects that combine traditional gaming values with the best of the mobile experience. Their turn-based roleplaying series SQUIDS, available for iOS, Android, PC, and Mac, has been enjoyed by more than one and a half million players worldwide. SQUIDS has also been made into a comic book series and is coming soon to television. Their upcoming brawler *Combo Crew* will release for iOS and Android in Q2 2013. To learn more, visit the company's website at http://thegamebakers.com.

Press release used courtesy of The Game Bakers

The press release starts with a catchy title that gives the most important details (game name, genre, developer name, platforms, "coming this spring"). This is followed by a subhead that expands on *Combo Crew*'s key features (modern yet old-school, asynchronous multiplayer across all platforms) and namedrops the developer's previous game.

The first paragraph starts with the developers' location, the date and the most important details of this announcement. If the reader stops reading after the first paragraph, you want them to take away the gist of the news (game name, genre, platforms, release timeframe).

The next three paragraphs give secondary information to summarize the game, establish the most important features and incorporate a quote from someone in the company. Don't expect press to repost your press release in its entirety (although some will), but do tell them everything they need to know to write up a brief news story about the game. If you were a potential customer reading about this game, what would get you excited about it? What features will you list on the game's store page? These are the types of details to include in your press release.

Press might pick up the quote verbatim for their news stories, so make it count! This is a good time to humanize the news with an anecdote (e.g., why you made this game, what you hope people will like about it). A press release doesn't need to have a quote, though, so if you feel like there's nothing more to say than you already have, you can leave it out. If relevant, quotes can also come from industry partners or other notable sources (for example, from another prominent indie developer).

Finally, the press release recaps where the game will be available. This information is less important before launch, since people can't go to those stores yet to buy the game, so in this press release it's at the bottom. In a press release announcing that a new game has just released, you'd probably want to list those channels closer to the top.

Typically, a press release ends with "boilerplate" paragraphs that describe the people or companies involved. This press release only has one such paragraph, "About The Game Bakers," but you can have more than one boilerplate paragraph if multiple studios or important people are involved.

Like pitch emails, a press release should be short and sweet at around 400–600 words. This is just one example; you can find more online and come up with a press release of your own that fits within this format but also makes sense for your game and your specific news.

When sending a press release, some press think it's rude or impersonal if you paste it into the email without any explanation. To avoid this, you can include a brief note at the top to ease the reader in to the news. Also, keeping in mind that the press release might be reposted in its entirety, you might have details that you want the press to know but don't want broadcast to potential customers, like that a beta preview build is available.

Here's the note that went with the *Combo Crew* announcement:
Hi [name],

The Game Bakers have been slaving away in the kitchen for months, and they're finally ready to share their newest concoction—*Combo Crew*! This is a totally unique beat 'em up game with asynchronous, platform agnostic co-op play . . . you've never played anything like it. *Combo Crew* will be out soon for iOS and Android devices, and the press release below has the scoop.

Combo Crew assets (artwork, logo, and video) can be downloaded from: http://thegamebakers.com/vip

If you'll be at PAX East, The Game Bakers would love to give you an early taste of *Combo Crew*. Please write back with a few times you could meet during show hours, and we'll set up an appointment.

Note used courtesy of The Game Bakers

Results

The *Combo Crew* announcement was picked up by major mobile gaming sites (including PocketGamer, Touch Arcade, AppSpy, and Modojo) as well as many multi-platform enthusiast sites, and the accompanying "over the shoulder" gameplay video was reposted by IGN. The press release was the first step in a PR campaign that went on to include in-person meetings at PAX East, distribution of about 200 review copies, and more than 100 reviews.

Note: Although press releases are common in the game industry, for indie games, less formal emails can work just as well. Like the novelty of speaking directly to the developer, informal (but still well-written and informative) emails can be a nice change of pace from the stiff corporate communications journalists often receive from large publishers.

Targeted Pitch Email

This less formal pitch email example is for SomaSim's Wild West–themed simulation game, *1849*. This game is set in existing towns around California that are historically linked to the Gold Rush, and we approached local newspapers to pitch this angle.

> Subject: Sacramento to be immortalized in "1849" video game, releasing soon—potential Sacramento Bee coverage?
>
> Hi [name],
>
> In 1849, Sacramento became part of American history during the Gold Rush—and on May 8 it will go down in video game history, too! I represent SomaSim, an independent San Francisco–based developer working on the Gold Rush–themed video game **1849**. As an entertainment reporter, would you like to check it out for the Sacramento Bee?
>
> **1849** is a simulation game in the style of the classic SimCity. Through 20 levels that take place in existing California towns (including Sacramento), players grow the local economy and balance citizens' needs against the backdrop of real Gold Rush scenarios and challenges. Should Sacramento be a mining town, a farming community, or a hub for trade? Will the pioneers flocking into town become productive prospectors or devolve into unruly drunks at the local saloon? That's your call!
>
> **1849**'s graphics were inspired by period photographs and surviving architecture. This trailer will give you an idea of how it looks and plays: https://www.youtube.com/watch?v=_q4Rs0tZOno
>
> More **1849** details are on the official website: http://www.somasim.com/1849
>
> With its focus on local history, **1849** is sure to interest the Bee's readers. The game will release May 8 for PC, Mac, iPad, and Android tablets—please let me know if you'd like a review copy for any of those platforms. If you want to hear more about the game and the locals who made it, they're available

for interviews either in person in San Francisco, or by email/
phone.

Thanks, I hope to hear from you!

Usage courtesy of SomaSim

Because this pitch went to press who normally wouldn't cover
video games, it describes the gameplay in ways even casual or
nongamers reading the local Sacramento newspaper can understand and relate to. We did namedrop the well-known *SimCity*, but
made an effort not to get too technical. Whoever you're reaching
out to, you want them to get the feeling this is a game they (and, by
extension, their readers) will be interested in hearing more about.
Sometimes that means geeking out with people who know the
game industry inside out, and sometimes it means describing your
game as you would to a relative who rarely plays games, but still
wants to know what you've been working on.

Results

This very targeted pitch, which went out to 20 newspapers, websites,
and radio stations in Northern California, was picked up by 8 of
them—that's a really good percentage! A similar pitch regarding a
Nevada-themed expansion pack yielded a review in *Nevada Magazine*.

Trade Show Meeting Pitch

When you go to a show like GDC, IndieCade, or PAX, it's a good
idea to set up press appointments ahead of time. Do this with a
targeted email that's relevant to the type of press attending the
show—for example, for a show like IndieCade you'd probably want
to focus on your experience and reputation as an indie developer,
while for GDC you could focus more on how your game fits into
the overall gaming landscape.

Here's a sample email inviting press to meet with Dave Gilbert of
Wadjet Eye Games at GDC, about a month before the final game in
Dave's acclaimed (but somewhat niche) *Blackwell* adventure game
series released.

Subject: GDC: Meet with Wadjet Eye Games to see final Blackwell adventure and talk about indie studio's future plans

Dear [name],

In 2006, Dave Gilbert released his first indie adventure game and unwittingly started a company. Eight years later, Wadjet Eye Games (http://www.wadjeteyegames.com) is going strong: this spring they'll conclude their long-running *Blackwell* mystery series, and new releases for iOS and PC are on the horizon. Want to meet with Dave in San Francisco to hear more?

Featuring an unusual "buddy cop" team—a spirit medium and the ghost who guides her—the *Blackwell* games are thoughtful point-and-click mysteries that have you helping New York City's recently dead cross over to the other side. At GDC, Dave can give you a **sneak peek of *The Blackwell Epiphany*,** the fifth and final Blackwell game coming to PC in April. Check out the trailer here for a taste of the storyline and atmosphere: https://www.youtube.com/watch?v=6ZLCm UiC7SQ

This acclaimed indie series will also come to iOS this spring, and at GDC you can get a **first look at** *The Blackwell Legacy* **on the iPad**—this will be Wadjet Eye's first time showing it to the press!

With *Blackwell* wrapped up, Wadjet Eye will spend 2014 **porting more of their back catalog to iOS and Android,** as well as **publishing two adventure games** for other indie devs. We haven't announced these games yet, so if you meet up at GDC you'll be one of the first to get the scoop.

Dave's best days to meet are Wednesday 3/19 thru Friday 3/21, but we might be able to squeeze you in Monday or Tuesday if those are your only available days. Please write back to suggest a few times that work for you during show hours.

Usage courtesy of Wadjet Eye Games

As usual, the email starts off with a strong subject line that lets the reader know what to expect. Putting the name of the show right up front lets press who are attending GDC know it's relevant to them.

Since GDC is a show that focuses on game development and includes developers all along the spectrum from small indies to huge AAA companies, the email starts off with a quick history of the company so the reader has an idea of what type of developer Wadjet Eye is. This first paragraph ends with a question that will hopefully prompt the reader to reply: "Want to meet?"

(This email was sent to the registered GDC press list, so we knew that the recipient would probably be there. If you're not sure the person you're emailing will be at the show, you could also start the paragraph with a question, e.g., "Will you be at GDC?")

The next three paragraphs detail what Dave would be discussing at GDC in order from most important to least important. If you're participating in a panel or exhibiting at the show, be sure to give details.

Since the email is fairly text heavy, we bolded the parts that describe what the reader could see at GDC, so this info would stand out. When press attend gaming shows their schedules tend to get pretty booked up, so you want to clearly state what special thing(s) you'll be able to show or talk about in person to make the meeting worth their while.

Finally, the email gives specific details about when meetings can take place, and a request to write back to book a time. When you confirm a meeting, include your cell phone number and a meeting spot, and ask for their cell phone number. You might even want to provide a photo of yourself—you don't want to miss each other in the crowd! If you're exhibiting (at a kiosk in the IGF Pavilion, for example), you can have the press meet you there, but it's still good to nail down a day and time so you're sure to be available and prepared when they show up.

Results

This particular mailing resulted in 15 in-person press meetings during GDC, with some people who were familiar with Wadjet Eye Games and others who had never heard about the studio before this. The mailing also boosted visibility for *The Blackwell Epiphany* leading into the game's launch, since the people Dave met with, as well as a few others who were unable to fit a meeting into their schedules, were later sent review copies.

Chapter 8
Marketing Materials

Indies have been consistently delivering extremely high levels of presentation polish and quality in their games.

When you start to create marketing materials, you should factor additional important considerations into the process beyond polish—in connection with marketing messaging and communication objectives. These materials should be more than just high-quality art in order to effectively build interest in your game.

Schedule time for creating marketing materials well in advance of launch—so you can get to the most effective executions, rather than inferior assets due to rushing.

Chapter Objectives:

- Identifying important elements to factor into the design process for creating effective marketing materials.
- Do's and Don'ts for key marketing materials.

GENERAL CONSIDERATIONS / GUIDELINES
Quick Read

Think about the key takeaway your marketing materials should deliver, in connection with the top messaging points for your game and marketing campaign. Viewers should be able to get these top points at a glance, through:

- **Legibility.** Your game name, tagline and key focus should come across clearly through your marketing materials.

  Some executions that get in the way of legibility: super intricate type of treatments with lots of visual flourishes, small text sizes, lengthy blocks of text and too many varying elements in the materials.

- **Determine Central Focus / Think about Weighting.** In approaching the materials, first identify what you want the intended central focus to be—main character(s), vehicle, tagline, etc. Executions that try to do too much without a central focus get muddled and then fail to effectively convey anything at all.

You can help direct the viewer's focus to the most important elements by determining how you weight them. Some visual elements should be larger, others smaller. Some should have lighter color values, others should have darker tones. Similarly, you can vary the size of different pieces of text—with the most important elements (e.g., the game name/logo) larger than others (tagline, release platforms).

> **Tip:** When the piece is completed, check back on the central focus you identified in the beginning to see if it delivered. Put the piece in front of colleagues and friends and ask what the top takeaway is for them. Iterate on the piece as needed to make it work!

- **Design for High Contrast.** In a nutshell, this refers to dark elements on a light background or light elements on a dark background—so the most important items pop!

  Too often, developers or publishers will post marketing materials that don't read well due to poor contrast. They may work as beautifully textured and nuanced scenes, but they don't effectively deliver the top, most important message to the target audience.

The design and layout on the next page direct the eye to the primary focus:

- Strong treatment for game name: high contrast—light colored text, rendered in bold strokes
- Tree limbs and branches frame and direct the viewer's eye to the central elements, along with the more subtle stepping-stone path
- The sunset and mountains provide a backdrop and bring further visual focus to the image's primary elements

This image from Infinite Fall's *Night in the Woods* effectively shows a number of key points as described in this section. Usage courtesy of Infinite Fall.

- This image also establishes the main character Mae the cat. Additional marketing materials from Infinite Fall build upon the iconically presented Mae as shown below.

Usage Courtesy of Infinite Fall.

- **Optimize for Format.** Some formats bring more constraints than others. For example, large-format key art on a banner at a trade show can achieve more than small format game icons in a mobile phone app store. Be sure to design for the limitations of the format, rather than trying to force the same art into every execution.
- **Audit the Field.** Take time to look at marketing materials for other games in the category: top sellers, comparable games and competitors. Identify what the best executions do well as a source of inspiration and what some do poorly to avoid the same mistakes. Make sure that your materials stand out and vary considerably from similar games.

Super Rigorous Fidelity: Yes or No?

People have different philosophies about whether you should or shouldn't move the in-game camera or game assets when capturing video and screenshots.

Some feel that you should only release screenshots or videos that show actual scenes exactly as they will appear in the final game when it releases.

Others will take liberties—moving the in-game camera to increase the drama, impact and presentation in the materials.

You will need to determine your position on this point. If you take liberties, make sure that the assets are not overly misleading, and do not create expectations that the game won't fulfill.

First Assets

The game's name and type treatment/logo will be the very first pieces of marketing content you'll create for your project.

As shown in this chapter's *Night in the Woods* example, your project can benefit by having a central image, key art or visual icon/symbol early on.

Game Name / Visual Treatment

For those who might not think of their game's name as marketing content—think again! The name is at the very center of the game's identity. It communicates core information about the project and is the single most frequently referenced element.

Important factors to consider as you're deciding on the game's name:

- **Title Length.** Consider how the title will appear in different storefronts. Short and catchy can work very well. Some storefronts automatically truncate long titles, which can lead to a letter jumble. If the game name must be long, think about possible catchy acronyms or nicknames.
- **Distinctiveness.** Is your title unique and distinctive, particularly in comparison to other comparable games in the category? Start by doing a web search for different game names you're thinking about.
- **Online Accounts.** Can you grab the URL, Twitter account, Facebook page, etc., associated with the proposed game name? If others have secured the online accounts for your proposed game name (or similar variations), would this possibly lead to confusion or make it more difficult for gamers to find information about your project?

  - When you identify a game name where you can lock in associated URLs and social media accounts, this can help tremendously for people seeking out information on the project. This can contribute to and reinforce your brand strength as well, particularly if you're considering expanding to a multi-game series.

- **Visual Presentation.** Mock up different types of treatments and/or draft logos to see how well potential names might read.

As you do this, think about how the visual treatment might appear in horizontal and vertical/square formats.

The Super	The Super
Confabulator	**Confabulator Gizmo**
Gizmo	
Vertical/Stacked Version	*Horizontal Version*

It can help to develop different title treatment variations up front—full color, white logo on black background, black logo on white/transparent background—and have these all available for download from your website.

> **Tip:** When you're evaluating different name options, consider the potential for misspellings. Some titles are more likely to lead to misspellings or typos, presenting challenges to interested gamers—as well as journalists!—looking for information on your game.

Be rigorous in maintaining consistency with your game name usages. If your game is called "SuperGame!," be sure to keep this consistent in all of your marketing materials—don't have it appear as "Super Game" sometimes, "Supergame" other times, and then "SUPERGAME!" elsewhere (different initial letter treatments, word spacing, punctuation, etc).

Central Image

Creating a central image for your game early on can help significantly in establishing a visual identity. Some examples:

- **Key Art.** Think in terms of key art from movies—the image that might appear first on a movie's website or teaser poster. This might be central characters in a heroic pose and locale or an interesting setting.

- **Symbol/Icon.** Some games have created cool iconic symbols that work very effectively as a central hook for the marketing campaign.

Marketing Assets: Key Goals

Be sure to identify the primary goal of each marketing piece before beginning, such as:

- Motivate visits to website for learning more
- Drive mailing list sign ups
- Generate video views
- Preorders
- Game purchases

These goals will vary at different stages of your campaign and for different kinds of marketing materials. Some marketing materials can work better for different goals than others (e.g., a video can achieve more, in an impactful way, than an icon in an app store).

Marketing Materials—Top Info

For many of your marketing materials, be sure to include the four top elements below clearly in your executions.

1. **Release timing**
2. **Planned platforms**
3. **Call to Action** (ties to goal as identified above)
4. **URL** (for getting more info)

When gamers view materials for a game that sounds interesting, these are the first things they want to know. Don't make them ask or hunt for this information. If you don't include it prominently, it will be among the first questions they'll ask or post: "Should I be looking for it within the next few months or next year?" "I play mainly on PC, is this game for me? Or is it mobile only?" Even if you don't have definitive information, it's better to include what you currently know rather than nothing.

As mentioned in Chapter 6, you're best off referring to a time of year, at first anyway (e.g., "Fall 20__"), and you can always modify this later as needed. For platforms, you could start with PC and Mac and indicate "more platforms expected" (if that's accurate).

For your call to action, pick one! You decrease the effectiveness and dilute the focus of the call to action by offering multiple options. So don't say: Come to our website, sign up for the mailing list, follow any of our extensive social media accounts, preorder and like us! Based on the stage you're at in the marketing cycle, identify the most appropriate call to action and have your marketing piece focus there.

So when you're posting content to the home page for your studio's website, creating videos, posters, flyers, etc., make sure these four elements appear clearly and prominently.

Videos

Players want to see gameplay first and foremost in your videos! Be sure to include lots of representative footage, showing what they'll actually be doing in the game. Mix up the footage as much as possible to show diversity and action-packed elements (if relevant for your game).

Sometimes, less is more—particularly for your first teaser videos. You can whet players' appetite, rather than hammer them with extended footage that might start to feel repetitive.

Beyond that, creative executions can vary. Some will include dramatic elements, builds and title cards for establishing the context. Others will lighten the mood and build affinity with humor.

Special attention to audio can prove very effective as well—killer music selections, well-synchronized visual/audio beats and dialog/voiceover.

Be sure to include the top four elements mentioned above in your video: release timing, planned platforms, call to action and URL.

Some games have released effective cinematic videos, with little to no gameplay. This can certainly generate strong interest and visibility. In these cases, you can plan for companion videos that show real gameplay.

As mentioned in Chapter 4, you can map out a series of videos that each focus on a different area of the project.

Screenshots

Your screenshots should show as much variety in the game as possible—different levels, characters, weapons, environments with different color palettes, etc. Review your proposed screenshots in a gallery to make sure they come across as diverse and varied.

When you release screenshots, posting batches of three to five or more at a time can work well, spread out over regular intervals—rather than saving up and posting huge batches all at once on a less frequent schedule.

Do

- Do show representative gameplay as much as possible— what players will do in the game, action-packed (if relevant for your game).
- Do think about the composition of your scenes, factoring in the general guidelines from the opening section of this chapter—legibility, contrast and weighting.

Don't

- Don't show the backs of characters (third-person games are a notable exception) or characters in static, uninteresting poses.
- Don't release batches of screens or footage that are nearly identical at a quick glance (nearly indistinguishable composition, color palettes, etc).

Icons

Icons are often the first visuals of the game that people see. In online store fronts and device-based app stores, these are essentially your packaging. The best icons stimulate interest and prompt for a closer look.

Stay cognizant of the format's constraints. Icons can display as small as 29 x 29 pixels in some views. This format does not work well for the kinds of high-detail textured images and compositions you might see in larger retail box formats.

Trying to include a strong iconic visual *and* the game name can be challenging in this small amount of real estate. You should generally choose one or the other, rather than try to include both.

Do's and Don'ts for Icons

Do

- Do feature a clear, succinct image in your icon that pops and conveys an interesting key element of the game.
- Do keep icon designs fairly simple and direct.

- Do design icons that focus on hero characters / "mascots" when relevant.
- If the title includes a strong brand or visual element, have your game icon focus there.
- Bright colors often work well (which doesn't need to mean garish).

Don't

- Don't try to cram too much into a small space. Icons generally can't (and shouldn't) try to do it all. If they try to do too much, they'll fail at all and create a muddled image.
- Don't overdo text in an icon. If the icon will have text, generally stick to one to two short words at most.

Store Pages

Short, succinct, compelling lines on your store page maximize impact and quick reads. Review quote snippets can work particularly well, e.g., "Editor's Choice!—IGN." Brief, bullet point, one liners also facilitate quick reads.

When you pick out review quote excerpts for your store pages, look carefully for the best ones to use. Ideally, you'll find snippets that convey helpful information about the game—so you'd include lines like "the best quick hit platformer this year with charming visuals I fell in love with . . ." rather than the less informative "it's great!"

Some marketing copy can create likeability with humor and personality (when appropriate for the subject matter).

Be aware of how much copy will display in different settings. Only the first line might show by default in an app store, for example, so make it a good one—like a review quote, award or compelling one-line game description. For this reason, make sure that the first line your prospective customers read isn't a disclaimer about system compatibility limitations or known issues you're working on fixing.

You can also make the most of the space available on your store page by including captions on your screenshots. You can call out different key features on each screenshot and/or highlight review quotes/awards on others.

Do's and Don'ts for Store Pages

Do

- Do have succinct, well-written text on your store page that sells your game effectively.
- Do make sure the store page reads quickly and clearly.

Don't

- Don't have super long walls of copy that are off-putting.
- Don't have typos, awkward wording or grammatical errors.

View in Context

As you start developing marketing materials for your game, be sure to think about where they'll be used. If you're creating an icon for iOS or Android, look closely at the different places this icon will appear—in different views of the relevant app store on various devices. If your game will release for smartphones, the views and icon sizes will vary from those on tablets and desktop app stores.

Here's one approach for determining how well your icon works: Open the icon in a picture viewing app and zoom far out until you're looking at the image at a very small size. If you've done a good job optimizing legibility and contrast, the icon will read well when zoomed far out. If not, this process should help in identifying areas for improvement.

Used courtesy of The Binary Mill.

Another helpful exercise: Paste your proposed icon into a screenshot of the online store environment where your game will appear. You might want to try this with a few variations of your icon to see which is working best. Having your mock-up include icons from comparable and competitive games can also help in determining the effectiveness of your icon.

Used courtesy of The Binary Mill.

Logo Soup

You'll periodically come across marketing materials with a rich delicacy of logo soup (or stew or mud!). As indicated in earlier portions of this chapter, too much content creates a messy muddle—same goes for logos. If you have a game that has the good fortune of winning multiple awards, pick the best ones to show visually, and possibly refer to others in text. If you have other required logos, do your best to spread them out (e.g., across multiple title cards if it's in video trailer format). This applies to overdoing different social media links as well.

Updating Marketing Materials

Once your game releases, be sure to update your marketing materials where possible. Add great review quotes, awards, Metacritic scores, game updates, etc.

You can add this information to the top of the store pages for your game and include them on screenshots in online stores, in updates to promotional videos, on your website, in materials you bring to trade shows and so on.

Recommended Exercises:

1. Create a first pass mock-up for your game's marketing materials incorporating recommendations, do's and don'ts from this chapter.

- If you're not an artist or designer, create simple line art or a schematic visual.

2. Test out your mock-ups with friends, family and colleagues.

   - Tune and refine as needed.
   - If you're not an artist or designer, have a skilled colleague or team member help you create more polished versions from your initial sketch.

3. If you've previously released games, review your marketing materials based on recommendations from this chapter.

   - Consider reworking these materials, incorporating new information from this chapter.

4. Assess marketing materials from games released by other developers.

   - Find examples that do and don't work well.

Chapter 9
Audience/Community Development

Connectivity through social media and devices continues to get better and better, and these advances provide outstanding ways to communicate directly and regularly with your audience. You can share information and content with them, engage and interact, and cut past layers and obstacles from prior eras and other channels. Given recent trends, this level of access should continue to improve in the coming years.

While PR, advertising, channel promotions and other kinds of programs can perform well—*you* can control and manage communications through the audience and community connections you build. As you get these started and expand their size, a portion of your marketing programs can then become quite a bit more straightforward to execute.

Chapter Objective:

This chapter reviews different kinds of audience development vehicles along with ways you can use and build them.

Tip: Your time and efforts in developing audience and community programs should reap significant rewards as you approach your first game's release date—and on into the future as well. These can become your most direct and unobstructed channels.

Personality and Tone

Before diving into channel specifics, let's review a few important related topics.

Most notably, the style and tone of communications with your audience play key roles in your community development.

Tip: A friendly, open, informal style works very well for creating affinity with your audience. You might find this more difficult at times, particularly when you run into challenges—technical glitches, game schedule delays, etc.

General rule of thumb: Keep cool, stay positive and be yourself. At times, you may need to step away from the computer and collect your thoughts before engaging.

An accessible communication style comes easily and naturally for some, less so for others. Be sure to find a person on your team who can work these channels effectively—or hire a part-time person that has strong skills in this area.

> **Tip:** Humor can work very well for building the connection and rapport with your audience. If you or your team have this in your arsenal, all the better!
>
> A light touch doesn't fit for all projects, particularly if it isn't appropriate for your style of game.

As with other communications covered in this book, you'll find that your audience will appreciate responsiveness and timeliness.

While communications on the internet can be challenging at times, with haters who love to hate, a balanced, rational communication approach can serve you best. Ultimately, taking the higher ground will cast you in the best light, particularly with prospective customers and members of the media who might be reading along—the kinds of people who matter most.

Your Website

Your website can present your games and studio with the highest level of fidelity—exactly how you want your audience to see them.

> **Tip:** While many have created super flashy websites, with bells, whistles and fireworks, you should think about function over form.

You can design your site with style and strong aesthetics, without funky web tech or gimmicks. Make it open and inviting, and have the most important information easily accessible. Simple can work quite well.

Web designers talk about having the most important information "above the fold" on each page. This term comes from the world of newspapers, referring to top content readers will see when they first get the periodical before unfolding it. For the web, this refers to having key content near the top of each page, which readers can see before needing to scroll down on a standard size monitor. Consider the increasing popularity of tablet devices for viewing websites when determining the monitor resolution you're designing for.

Your home page should present visitors with the most essential content clearly and prominently.

Key Facts: Top Level Importance for the Home Page on Your Website

Information on Your Latest Game

- **Game name**
- **Platform(s)**
- **Expected release timing**
- **Distribution channels**

Many don't lock in some information until closer to the game's release date, which is ok.

Consider TBA (To Be Announced) for your unknown information, rather than TBD (To Be Determined). TBD could imply you have no idea where you'll land, and this may be accurate at times. You can project a different impression with TBA: "We're working on exciting plans, which we'll share soon. Stay tuned!"

Your pricing information can post closer to the game's release date.

Additional Content Recommendations for Your Website:

- **Engaging central feature** to draw viewers in and prompt interest in your game—such as a compelling splash image or video.
- **Timely news and project updates** in a clear location on your home page—perhaps a side column with headlines or capsule summaries, linking visitors to a blog page for additional information. Look for ways to present this so that visitors can quickly identify the newest and most current information on your project at a glance from your home page.
- **Prominent links for building engagement**—to your Facebook page, Twitter account, YouTube channel, RSS feed.
- **Email mailing list sign up prompt**
- **Links to "About" and "Press" sections**

- **About:** for more information about your studio, team, game(s)
- **Press:** to assist journalists with covering your game—including contact info, key assets for download and possibly links to article highlights

- **Detail pages for individual game(s)**

A website stats tool can prove invaluable for tracking traffic as you ramp up your game launch, to assess how different initiatives increase visitors and interest at your site and to assist with evaluating program performance.

Email

Everyone's email mailing list starts small. The earlier you start your list sign ups, the better off you'll be down the line.

In the initial stages of your studio, you'll likely have a small online presence with moderate communication frequency. As you grow and begin to generate interest, you can start building one of your first valuable marketing resources by inviting people to join your mailing list. If you attend a trade show, get your project covered on an industry blog or website, generate interest through social media, and more; your mailing list helps to capture leads and establish this foundation for direct communications with your audience.

As your mailing list size expands, think about ways to keep this connection going through regular email communications—perhaps monthly. People choose to join your mailing list because they *want* to hear from you! So this is not spam, and it's not crass to have a mailing list of people who sign up by their own choice. Ultimately, this can become one of your best vehicles—your top, most engaged, informed, fervent enthusiasts and supporters. Journalists and industry contacts may sign up for your mailing list, so this can help with those kinds of efforts as well.

If all goes well—with interesting, engaging content in emails to your base about projects your fans enjoy—subscribers will forward your emails along to others.

Ways to Build Your Mailing List

- **Mailing list sign up prompt.** Post a mailing list sign up box in prominent places—on your website's home page, game page, Facebook page, perhaps even in your game's main menu screen. The game's purchase page is another solid place to prompt people to join your mailing list.

- **Communicate benefits.** In places where you post your mailing list registration field, clearly convey benefits of signing up—timely news, perhaps periodic special offers, and more.
- **List-building initiatives.** Consider periodic promotions for building your mailing list, and make sure the offers are relevant. For example, offer discount coupons for one of your previous games (or a colleague's comparable game) for all who join your mailing list during a specified period. Or arrange for a giveaway selected at random for all who join the mailing list during a predefined window.

The case study following this chapter provides an interesting list-building example.

Social Media Channels

Social media have been evolving as effective ways to communicate with your audience—with advantages to other channels in some areas.

> **Tip:** The more ways you can offer to connect with your community, the better. Some in your audience prefer to spend their time on Twitter and consume information there. Others gravitate to Facebook, or elsewhere. Have your communications tuned to your audience's preferences.

Creating and posting prominent links to these social channels help to build the size of the universe you can communicate with directly—for when you're preparing new game announcements, new content releases, special offers and more.

Once you've got these channels created and have established a base of followers, be sure to post there regularly. A Twitter or Facebook link from your website that you don't post to doesn't do anyone any good. Weekly updates can work well, with increased frequency during more active times—such as the buildup to a new content release. Be sure to include URLs in your tweets and posts, to make it as easy as possible for interested followers to find information you're posting about.

Followers and fans also generally appreciate when you mix up the kinds of pieces you post—info that could be of interest for them, topical perspectives and more—not just product and sales information.

As with mailing lists, you can field promo campaigns to build up the number of your followers. For example, The Binary Mill ran a campaign in its *Gun Club* mobile app, which offered a free weapon to any that followed their social media pages. The studio launched a dedicated new Facebook page as part of this campaign, which grew from zero to several hundred thousand within a few months. These followers were relatively qualified, in that they were going for an add-on reward to extend the app they're interested in, rather than for a random prize like a new iPod or tablet or game console.

Used courtesy of The Binary Mill

Community Forums

Adding a forum section to your website can work well for building connections with your fans and getting them engaged. You and your team can also interact with people through other kinds of forums, like the ones run by online game distribution channels.

When you can interact with the audience in the comments sections of articles about relevant topics on your games, that can resonate too. Personality and tone play important roles in these communications. Stay friendly and positive.

Online Video Channels

Chapter 4 talked about planning for videos at key stages of your launch buildup: teasers, gameplay, features, your full launch trailer and possibly more. In addition to the impact of this medium, video channels work well for building your audience, affinity, engagement and interest.

Developers and content creators will continue to come up with interesting new uses for video. These include:

- Live streaming days, to give an inside look at your game development as it progresses—perhaps every week, month or somewhere in between
- Streaming sessions that showcase players
- Spotlights of head-to-head multiplayer sessions from the community
- User-created content and/or contests
- Other creative ideas that you have!

Additional Audience Development Initiatives

Continually look for new ways to build your audience base and get more supporters.

For example:

- **Contests**—for great user-generated content, multiplayer showdowns and random giveaways.
- **Fan art**—posting galleries and praise for great submissions.

Communication Channel Matrix

Table 9.1

Vehicle	Well suited for	Recommended frequency and timing during active periods (building to new game release)
Website/Blog	Longer form content posts	One to multiple times per week
Email	Shorter text, can link to longer content on website and/or videos, downloads	Monthly
Twitter	Short, snappy posts Super timely, micro communications	Multiple posts throughout day when possible
Facebook	Timely posts, generally less micro than Twitter Can be longer than Twitter, but not overly lengthy	Multiple posts throughout day, daily, or multiple times during week
Video	Presenting your game in motion Showing rather than telling Prepare features on your game development as it progresses Live streaming sessions	Generally at key stages as you build towards launch—a number of videos, with the biggest one(s) right around launch time

Additional tips:

- **Images prompt engagement.** Compelling art, screenshots, photos and graphics capture viewers' attention and can drive responses and clicks. Be sure to integrate these into your communications.
- **Break up text with headers, bullets, captions and call outs.** These can help with skimmability and encourage people to read more of your post. Some will bounce away when faced with large blocks of text.
- **Stay up to date with these channels as they evolve and new ones as they emerge.**

Recommended Exercises:

1. Create an audience development plan for your studio—including core vehicles described in this chapter as well as new ones that might be emerging now.
2. Write three sample posts: one based on your game project, one based on other games you're playing/you like and one based on a relevant topic in the category.
3. Determine how your website may or may not address recommendations from this chapter and consider making adjustments.

Case Study: Telltale Games

Building the Base

A "house list" of enthusiasts who opt in to your email mailing list can become a valuable asset for your studio, generating stronger and stronger returns as the list—and your organization—grow. In the earliest days of San Francisco Bay Area–based Telltale Games, the team pursued a number of initiatives for building this list, which soon contributed to positive gains for new game announcements, launches, sales, audience development, cross-selling and other programs.

Established in 2004 with a focus on a new model for the industry—"seasons" of rich story-driven game episodes, inspired by broadcast and print-based serialized content—Telltale began with enthusiast franchises: Jeff Smith's popular *Bone* comic series and Steve Purcell's *Sam & Max*.

Telltale began the email list-building process early on, with prominent sign up links on the website's home page and game pages. Also, the purchase path for games and merchandise included a mailing list subscription prompt, checked "yes" by default (customers could easily choose to uncheck this). Telltale delivered on the value of sign ups with consistent mailings: regular monthly newsletters and off-cycle mailings for relevant news—big announcements, launches, special offers and more.

To drive mailing list subscriptions higher, Telltale fielded a number of targeted programs, highlighted by an impactful execution in connection with Talk Like a Pirate Day and the studio's pirate-themed *Tales of Monkey Island* series. For those unfamiliar with Talk Like a Pirate Day, it started with friendly banter between friends. It soon became an international meme each September 19, where hordes of people tweet and post piratey sayings on their websites, along with many other peculiar celebrations. Telltale took this opportunity to craft a promotion based on *Tales of Monkey Island* and this event—which also benefited from flexibility provided by the episodic game model. The program in broad strokes:

- Telltale set up a "Play Like a Pirate" landing page for visitors to get a free *Monkey Island* game episode to celebrate Talk Like a Pirate Day. Interested players needed only to submit their email addresses so Telltale could send them their activation key.
- The registration page provided an option to join the Telltale mailing list, for special offers on additional *Monkey Island* game episodes and more.

Talk Like a Pirate Day became a peak traffic day at the Telltale website up through this point, along with high milestones for email registrations and other metrics. Importantly, this program provided a relevant offer for qualified prospective customers. People interested in registering to get a free *Monkey Island* game are more likely candidates for Telltale games than if the company offered free iTunes or Amazon gift cards, for example.

New customers from this promo converted well on follow-up mailings—for more games as well as *Monkey Island* merchandise and other series from Telltale. Telltale later fielded additional programs with the same set up—e.g., register to get a free game from an earlier *Sam & Max* season, as part of buildup for launching the new *Sam & Max* season.

Concluding Notes

Like every new organization, Telltale and its audience development started small. Through ongoing programs and initiatives, the studio achieved substantial growth to its mailing list and other metrics. For mailings to its audience, Telltale developed fun, interesting and engaging content in the form of a newsletter called "The Interloper," which parodied tabloid newspaper periodicals. The Interloper features included information on the games and studio in the form of articles, interviews and features, such as an "Ask Max" advice column and even recipes. With an approach that built customer affinity rather than just sell, sell, sell, Telltale provided content that resonated with its audience as the company and mailing list pursued growth. The newsletters included clear information on new game releases, special offers and merchandise sections as well. Soon, the emails consistently generated revenue bumps in connection with each mailing.

Chapter 10
Post-Launch

Marketing for your game shouldn't end when it launches. By developing post-release sustaining marketing programs, you can extend your game's revenue stream, rather than promptly closing the book on the project. You should map out these initiatives while developing your game's full marketing plan—well before the launch date. Your plan can go after a more prosperous long tail, rather than a short burst and flame out.

Chapter Objectives:

- Identify important post-release areas of focus for your project.
- Determine ways to extend the sales curve for your games and generate additional revenues.

Immediately after Launch

In the hours immediately following your game releases, you and your team will want to breathe a huge sigh of relief. Go ahead! You've earned it! Whew!

Then, jump on important post-launch follow-up.

Reviews / Coverage Follow-Up with Press

Work with journalists, bloggers, Let's Players, etc., to get coverage of your game posted for building interest. It's important to include post-release outreach in your plans, following up from the period before launch. As described earlier in this book, you may not get traction with your first communications to influencers. They're busy, with pitches from lots of different game contacts, so stay with it!

Tip: Don't take a pushy or impatient approach in your follow-up, like "When will you review my game?" or "Why haven't you posted your article yet?" Reviewers don't respond well to this.

You can follow up with people about a week after sending review code, for example:

"I hope you've had a chance to check out [game name] and are enjoying it so far. Please let me know if there's anything I can help with or any questions you might have."

As favorable reviews come online, incorporate these into your communications to continue building momentum—post links/great quotes/ Metacritic scores to your online store pages, blog, Facebook, retweets, the works. You can also include these in your ads, videos and other marketing materials. You should contact the journalist or publication editor to ask them if it's ok to use their quote in this context. Most appreciate this additional visibility for their byline, site or magazine.

Social Media

Stay active on social media as your game launches and immediately thereafter—posting links to strong coverage, fan reactions, gameplay tips, fun content from players and more. This too can help build visibility and momentum for your game in these first important days and weeks.

Game Support

Keep an eye on indicators of your game's stability and performance, particularly in the initial hours and days after it releases—customer posts at online distribution channels, forums, comments in reviews, emails to the support email address you set up, etc. Importantly, keep the tone of responses friendly and constructive to help players with any issues they might run into. Be prepared to promptly release a bug fixing or compatibility update shortly after launch if needed.

Positive customer experiences in these initial post-launch days and weeks play an important role in the brand-building process for your studio.

> **Tip:** High levels of responsiveness and customer satisfaction can contribute to positive perceptions and word of mouth. Lags and neglect can do the opposite, undermining the long hours your team has put into game development.

Product Life Cycle

Management professionals refer to the "product life cycle" when approaching the business planning process for their organizations. This covers the path from introduction and growth through maturity, and then, frequently, saturation and decline.

In some categories, such as entertainment and gaming, teams can craft a variety of approaches for extending a game's life span and boosting run rates periodically. These include:

New Content Additions

New content can help to build affinity with existing players and also attract interest with new players. This often comes in the form of paid add-ons—downloadable content (DLC) or in-app purchases (IAP). Be sure to consider strategic free updates as well, with the goal of driving engagement, not just immediate revenues.

Content additions can include new characters, levels, weapons, skins, story extensions, you name it. The subject matter for some new additions might come from timely tie-ins (e.g., seasonal or topical themes) and others might come from high-quality creations from the player community.

- You might want to look for opportunities to bundle packets of new content together and expand from a minor update to a more sizable release—e.g., to a version 1.5 or 2.0. You can field a marketing campaign around this kind of release to generate additional interest from gamers, while increasing the potential for a new wave of attention through press coverage and channel partner promos.
- Be sure to coordinate dates for new content releases with your price promotion plans. You can extend sales at your highest price with new content, rather than giving customers more for less by releasing your update at the same time as a major sale.

Planned Promotions

As you develop the post-release marketing plans for your game, map out promotions that you can run at different times—perhaps beginning 3 to 6 months after launch. If the game performs below your projections when it launches, then you might want to field your first promotion earlier rather than later.

Be thoughtful in your planning, and plot out an orchestrated timeline of different kinds of promotions throughout the life cycle—seasonal promotions with relevant content and possibly discounts, weekend sales, holiday offers, milestone promos (XX,000 units, one-year anniversary), and so on.

Community-Driven Programs

Your community can help with sustaining interest for your game after it releases. These core fans can spread positive word of mouth with friends and share their enthusiasm. Some ways your team can contribute to this:

• **User-Generated Content**

Some games offer ways for players to create new content—new levels, skins, mods, etc. This can keep the game fresh and interesting, with the community extending your game's ideas far beyond the resources of your team. User-generated additions often bring unique and custom content, specially tailored for different groups.

You might even get player-generated content that's so strong that you'd want to work with the contributors to integrate their innovations into future releases of the core game, DLC packs or updates.

• **Contests**

Contests can also work well for building interest and audience engagement after launch.

User-generated content fits well for contests, with prizes for top contributions. You can also create different kinds of contests beyond user-generated content, such as:

- Best fan art/fan fiction
- Best player-created videos based on game content
- Best cosplay based on game characters
- Head-to-head showdown competitions (for multiplayer games)
- Prizes for top players in leaderboards (weekly/monthly)

Build engagement by sharing news on finalists and winners through your website and social network. When these kinds of programs perform best, finalists and winners post about them within their networks.

Pricing

As you work through the planning process for your game and its product life cycle, think also about how this relates to the pricing strategy. Again, other kinds of businesses can provide helpful input.

Pricing for movies and books, for example, typically start with premium pricing at launch time—for the most engaged consumers who are least price sensitive, willing to pay more to get the hottest and freshest when it first becomes available.

Then, after launch, prices come down. Movies migrate to second-run theaters and channels with lower prices. Similarly, prices for books decrease as they move from hard cover to paperback—and then get further discounted with back-catalog pricing.

Don't think about this as a "race to zero," and resist any impulses you might have to go after quick, deep and frequent price cuts for trying to stimulate run rates. Rather, develop the full life-cycle pricing strategy for your game well in advance, and stick with it as much as possible—full price/intro time, planned promotions, mid-life and late-life price adjustments.

> **Tip:** By reducing prices for earlier games from your studio when you announce or release a new one, you can generate incremental revenues. Lower prices for earlier games also helps to stimulate trial and build the base—which can translate into higher sales levels for your new game when it releases.

Additional Post-Launch Considerations

Awards

Be sure to submit your games for awards programs and competitions. You can get an additional visibility and sales bump by getting your game listed as a nominee or finalist, even if it doesn't win. And consider a price promotion when finalists get announced, to build on the awareness boost and drive incremental sales for those curious to check out the game that's gaining acclaim.

Merchandise

Tie-in merchandise can work well for some games and series—those that attract a following, have characters that lend themselves to merch, generate catchy phrases, etc. Merch programs can be relatively easy to set up with local vendors, turn-key e-commerce websites and minimal part-time staffing. When merchandising programs fit for your game, they can not only help in building out the strength of your franchise, they can also generate incremental revenues for your business.

Series

Developing follow-up games can assist with establishing your studio, game catalog, audience and critical mass. If the first game generates strong sales, you'll have pre-existing awareness and customers for a follow-up.

Some have developed sequels for games that didn't get to high sales volumes—advancing gameplay and storylines from a foundation started in an initial game, and building greater interest and sales for the follow-up.

You can begin development, communications and ongoing audience growth for a multi-game series shortly after releasing the first game—particularly while awareness is relatively high.

Library / Back Catalog

As you grow, your studio establishes a back catalog and library of games.

Your marketing plans can include initiatives related to your first game while promoting your second. For example, you can reduce the price of your first game at the time of your second game's announcement. This provides an option for interested gamers to check out your studio's projects and see how they like them—building the base for your new title when it releases. This can work for games that are not directly related to each other in a series, as well as for sequels and follow-ups.

As your studio and catalog grow, you can create pricing tiers across your games—with the earliest releases at the most inexpensive price point A, later titles at mid-tier price point B and the freshest newest games selling at a premium, at price point C.

You can also create bundles, with discounts for customers who purchase multiple games in your library.

Recommended Exercises:

1. If your current game has not been set up for post-release extensibility, identify ways that you can approach this for your next game.
2. Draft three different kinds of post-release promotions for your game.

Case Study: Flippfly's
Race the Sun

Making Lemonade from Lemons and the Long Tail

Wisconsin-based Flippfly has run counter to some past assumptions in the category. First, the studio established its business in the American Midwest, in an area populated by fewer indie developers than other parts of the country. And second, Flippfly has continually built the base of customers for its *Race the Sun* game in the months after launch—rather than within the first days and weeks of the game's initial release.

Usage courtesy of Flippfly, LLC

  While *Race the Sun* may not map to a textbook launch plan, the team's tenacity, persistence and energy helped drive a sustained sales ramp increase and long tail.

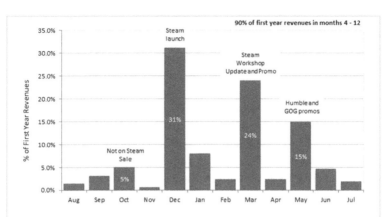

Race the Sun's first-year sales, broken out by the percentage of revenues earned each month.

Usage courtesy of Flippfly, LLC

Race the Sun's initiatives included:

- **Spring:** Kickstarter with a moderate $20,000 goal, 108% funded.
- **Early Fall:** Game release on PC and Mac, with purchasing available only through e-commerce widget on Flippfly website.
- **Mid-Fall:** Game promotion, approximately six weeks after launch, helps drive Steam Greenlight process and unit sales bump. Distribution also expanded to include GOG.com at this time.
- **Winter:** Launch on Steam.
- **Following Spring:** Update to game, adding support for Steam Workshop and Linux, coordinated promotion campaign.

And then, they made continuing plans for new promotions, new platform releases and updates.

Brothers Aaron and Forest San Filippo are the principals behind Flippfly, with Aaron providing his experience from AAA development teams and Forest bringing business and design expertise. They created *Race the Sun* as a different kind of endless runner game, where the player pilots a solar-powered craft, racing against the sunset at breathtaking speed. The game includes continuing varied terrain through procedurally generated landscapes, co-op multiplayer, and more.

When the game first released, it did not have a mass channel in place, as the game was working its way through the Steam Greenlight process at this time. Interested customers could purchase the game through a Humble widget on the Flippfly website.

The team posted a launch recap on its site and Gamasutra shortly after launch, with the headline "A Month after Launch, Losing Steam." The article relayed underperforming sales numbers, lessons learned and theories—highlighting distribution channels as a key area of concern for their team. In addition to sharing hard-earned experiences with other indies, the articles and posts continued to build visibility and awareness for Flippfly and the game.

Flippfly continued to persevere, staying active on social media, talking up the game and seeding the game in the community. They also reached out to press and influencers of all sizes— journalists, bloggers, YouTubers with moderate followings, and more. The game got its biggest early traffic, sales and Greenlight spike a month after launch from coverage on a YouTube channel with high viewership, rather than from traditional press outlets. Aaron's recommendation: "Above all, don't give up. Sometimes it takes months of hard work before people start taking notice of your game—this is the new norm in a world where dozens of quality indie games are released every month."

The team then landed on another way to make lemonade from lemons—conceiving and deploying the "Not on Steam Sale." Posted to a site created by Flippfly, this promotion inspired by Steam's big sales brought together dozens of games working their way through the Greenlight system, including *Race the Sun*. For games in the promotion, the site included (a) attractive discounts, (b) e-commerce widgets from Humble for direct purchases and (c) links to the game's Greenlight page. This strong campaign theme and execution also generated press interest, which resulted in coverage on a number of gaming sites. During the course of the promotion, *Race the Sun* and several other games in the program exceeded the Greenlight voting threshold—and achieved notable unit sales increases.

With the Steam channel slot secured, Flippfly prepped its next wave for *Race the Sun*. The team created a new trailer and press push for the Steam launch, which it deployed before the end of the year.

After the holiday break, Flippfly continued to drive for the long tail, developing additional plans for *Race the Sun*. Notably, the team added Steam Workshop and Linux compatibility for the game. Steam supported the new Workshop release with a feature slot on the home page. As this new version released, Flippfly ran a promotional discount along with a contest for the best user-created content. The team also developed additional platform plans for *Race the Sun* on PlayStation, Vita and Oculus Rift at this time.

Concluding Notes

Race the Sun provides an excellent example of a studio grabbing success from the jaws of defeat. Despite challenges, underperforming sales levels and disappointment in the earliest days of the game's release, Flippfly found a number of ways to make lemonade from lemons, go after the long tail, and generate positive returns for *Race the Sun*. This all contributed to a strong starting point and seed funding for the studio's next game, which it designed and prototyped during this period.

Chapter 11
What If Something Goes Wrong?!

What should you do if something goes wrong? It very well might.

A Murphy's Law reportedly referenced in the military states "No battle plan survives contact with the enemy."

Prepare carefully and diligently, yet stay nimble and ready for course changes and adjustments as needed.

In decades of marketing games and technology, this author has had numerous plans that have executed differently than their original timeline and assumptions—and many don't launch with their revised timelines either!

Plan for Flexibility

You should keep yourself and your team open to changes while developing and executing your plans. Building buffers into your schedules can help—and larger buffers can prove particularly beneficial.

Games often take longer to complete than originally anticipated. Or you may have ideas for improving your game midway through development, which can increase its potential for success considerably. Market variability, evolving audience tastes and new platform/channel opportunities can also arise, calling for a course change. Or, you may decide to shift your release date to take advantage of a marketing program—an event, promotional opportunity or partner alliance. Again, be flexible!

If Disaster or "The Unexpected" Strikes

You may experience a seemingly catastrophic calamity during the course of your project. Think about ways to make lemonade from lemons, and you'll find ways to salvage many kinds of "disasters." As an example, the Flippfly case study in this book shows how one developer persevered after running into challenges. Hopefully this can help you keep some perspective—launches often do not play out as originally conceived, and you should respond by developing alternative plans as needed.

Concluding Thoughts

When marketers get prompted by the question "Is marketing an art or a science?" the answer will often be "both!" While marketing tracking systems, metrics and new technologies continue to emerge, variability remains. In gaming and entertainment, we have additional wild cards—with subjectivity in connection to game content, audience tastes and intangibles. As referenced early in this book, marketing plans vary considerably for each game and situation. Stay tenacious, diligent and persistent! Field marketing programs, evaluate them, make refinements, and then iterate.

Also notable in this field—we're all consumers of marketing campaigns, and many of us for game content. As you move through your days, take note of marketing pieces that work well for you and look for inspiration across many different product categories—film, television, consumer electronics, cars, household items and more.

Please be sure to check out the Appendices at the end of this book. They include additional resources and worksheets, which should help with your marketing endeavors.

Lastly, continue to stay active and vigilant. Be on the lookout for evolving trends and opportunities. Supplement takeaways from this book with online resources and searches—including materials, articles and links posted at the author's website www.theindiemarketer.com.

Best wishes to all of you on your projects and marketing programs. You can reach out through the links on my website above and let me know how it goes!

Appendix 1
Glossary

Assets—content used for presenting the product to influencers through marketing materials; refers specifically to screenshots, videos, key art, logos, etc.

Brand / Branding—unique identity, personality and characteristics for attracting and retaining loyal customers.

Breakeven—threshold where product earnings reach the level of the total product development investment; breakeven calculations often include investments related to prototyping/research, marketing, sales, distribution and operation costs.

Bundle—when different items get combined together in an attractive, high-value package, e.g., multiple products sold together in a bundle; product + "making of" / concept art book + original soundtrack, etc.

Call to Action—the trigger line or "button" in marketing materials, prompting for the next step by interested consumers, e.g., "get trial version," "preorder now," "buy now."

Channel (distribution)—place where products are available for purchase (e.g., App Store, Amazon, Steam).

Fundamentals—core building blocks that provide a foundation for the marketing plan development process, to help tackle how one will first approach specific key marketing considerations.

Key Art—typically high resolution, carefully composed representative image that can consistently represent the product across marketing materials, such as websites, posters, online stores, etc. (key art is analogous to movie poster art for films).

Landing Page—page on studio's website where marketing vehicles direct interested customer prospects. Landing pages should include important content such as product descriptions, channels, release timing and compelling visual assets.

Launch—product release time; term commonly used in connection with a sizable buildup and fanfare for the release.

Library (also called Back Catalog)—prior product releases from the company, which they can continue to market and monetize.

Long Tail—when companies develop product marketing plans to focus efforts on maintaining interest, revenues and engagement for a sustained period of time; contrast from short burst programs that build to a peak and then abruptly end.

Media—often used to refer to "press"; can also be used to describe different kinds of assets (media types) such as videos, screenshots, key art, etc.

Media Alert—form of press communication, more informal than a press release; media alerts are often short news updates, presented in conversational tone rather than tighter business style of press release.

Messaging—verbiage used to communicate publicly about the product across different kinds of media, tuned and refined to get to the most effective, succinct and impactful wording.

Ps (Four Ps)—*Product* (details, features), *Price* (how much the product sells for), *Promotion* (ways the product is promoted and marketed) and *Place* (distribution outlets for selling the product).

Pitching—the process of reaching out to key influencers—typically press, publishers, industry figures—to build interest in the product.

Positioning / Positioning Statement—how your product compares to/differs from other products in your target market—its "position" on the landscape and in the consumer's mind. The positioning statement is the concise, specific wording used to describe a product's positioning.

Press Kit (Media Kit)—a press kit brings together key information for journalists to help them write about your game, often in an online format like a web page—including the game description, platforms, release dates, logos, screenshots, videos and so on.

Press Release—form of press communication, using a very specific format, typically for big announcements.

Product Life Cycle—a product's path from introduction and growth through maturity, and often saturation and decline; term used in the business planning process.

Promotions—programs for raising visibility and driving interest, often through structured initiatives; these can take the form of price promotions (discount offers) or other kinds of promotions (such as bundles, giveaways, channel/store promotions).

ROI (Return On Investment)—measure of profitability; calculated by subtracting the cost of an initiative from the income generated by the initiative, and then dividing the resulting amount by the cost of the initiative [(income – cost) / cost]; can be used as a metric for comparing performance of different kinds of alternative programs.

Seasonality—trends and market performance characteristics at different times of year or "seasons"; e.g., one can assess sales trends during the holiday season in comparison to summer or spring.

Social Media—vehicles and platforms for user-created content, sharing and communities—e.g., Twitter, Facebook.

Sustaining—post-launch marketing initiatives for continuing to generate interest in the product after the big launch buildup phase.

Tagline—well-crafted, punchy one-liner that helps generate interest in the product.

Target Audience—specific group of customers that an organization focuses on for its products and marketing initiatives—those most likely to buy; audience definition based on key characteristics such as demographics, tastes, interests and more.

USP / Universal Selling Proposition—makes a unique proposition to the customer, not merely hyperbole or empty words; is clearly differentiated from competitors, and is compelling in order to drive interest and purchases.

Vehicle—refers in general terms to different forms of marketing, such as paid banner ads, email campaigns, social media, videos, etc.

Appendix 2
Marketing Fundamentals Worksheet

Whether you market your game yourself or work with outside specialists, this worksheet can help you crystallize key points in preparation for your full plan development. Chapter 2 covers concepts from this sheet in detail. If you work with an outside specialist and complete this worksheet for them in advance, they will benefit greatly from this prep work.

Your Elevator Pitch

Concise description of your game that you can deliver "within the time of a typical elevator ride"

Positioning Statement

How you position your game relative to other games in your target market; addresses how your game might compare to or differ from other games

---

Unique Selling Proposition

What makes this game special

Style of Game

Type of gameplay, genre

Target Audience

Who you expect will be the primary audience for this game—audience description, demographics, characteristics

---

Price

Estimated price for game, pending finalization or possible adjustment before launch

---

Product

What this product is, including key features

Promotion

Ideas for how you'll promote this game—which you'll continue to develop throughout the marketing plan creation process

---

Place

Planned distribution channels—e.g., mobile app stores, Steam, digital console channels

---

Planned Platforms

Specific desktop, mobile, console platforms planned—initial and possibly post-release platforms

Platforms for initial launch date:

Post-launch platforms (and approximately how long after launch):

Planned Release Timing

When you are currently planning to complete and release the game

---

Game Performance Targets

Breakeven Income and Associated Unit Volume

Unit Sales Goals

Good

_____

Better

_____

Best

_____

Revenue Goals

Good

_____

Better

_____

Best

_____

Estimated Marketing Spending Budget

_____

Pursue Publisher or Self-Publish?

_____

Marketing lead(s)

Which team member (if any) will drive marketing, or outside resource(s) to pursue

_____

Appendix 3
Marketing Plan Outline

The paragraphs below describe key content and sections for organizing your game's marketing plan.

Set Up / Situation Analysis

The marketing plan can begin with setup information—relevant background briefing and analysis on the project, team, studio, series, market category, lead platform(s) and other pertinent information.

Fundamentals

The plan can then move into addressing key fundamental marketing points—per the Fundamentals worksheet in the preceding appendix and Chapter 2.

Key Goals

Including sales performance targets and other possible strategic goals in the plan helps to keep the focus on the most important areas—for crafting initiatives to address top objectives and for getting the team's efforts aligned. These goals can include numbers needed to achieve breakeven.

Strategy

The strategy section articulates the underlying framework for the marketing plan and programs. For example, will marketing emphasize PR or social media based on characteristics of the game and/or development team that you expect to resonate with different audiences? Alternatively, perhaps the team will devise a strategy based on key partners involved with the project or new technology/platforms showcased by the game or early release on new/emerging devices.

Timeline

The plan should include timelines for different elements of the plan—announcements, programs for different kinds of vehicles (e.g., PR, social media, paid), key events, and so on.

This helps with developing your marketing resource plans—when you will need important assets such as a landing page, screenshots, videos, playable game builds for shows, preview/review code, and so on.

The timeline will cover dates leading up to launch, the launch window (two to four weeks before launch up through the release date) and post-launch.

Plan Details—by Vehicle

As you determine the appropriate focus for your game's marketing and which kinds of programs will work best, your plan can then map out specifics for each vehicle you'll use—PR strategies, social media tactics, and so on. It can help to break out separate sections for different important vehicles.

Post-Launch / Sustaining Plans

The plan should extend through the post-launch period, so the game can go after the long tail with a series of sustaining programs and initiatives.

Additional

The outline above can prove helpful, particularly for studios developing their first plans on their own. More detailed marketing plans can include additional detail, as the studio's efforts get more sophisticated and the game marketing stakes ramp up—such as:

- SWOT Analysis (Strengths, Weaknesses, Opportunities, Threats)
- Competitive Analyses
- Market Analysis
- Market Segmentation

Appendix 4
Checklists

Key Information for Most Marketing Materials

The section below provides a handy checklist of information to include in most marketing materials—your studio's main website, game pages, videos, signage at trade shows and so on.

[ ] Game name
[ ] Studio name
[ ] Planned platforms
[ ] Expected release timing
[ ] URL for more information

Scale content based on format. For example, you might also include a game description one-liner for signage at a show. For your website, you would include a longer game description and feature bullets. If you're marketing in a channel that requires a rating, your materials should include that where needed as well.

Key Information for PR Materials

For media alerts, press releases, pitch emails, etc.

[ ] Game name
[ ] Studio name
[ ] Game description / feature bullets
[ ] Planned platforms
[ ] Expected release timing
[ ] URL for more information
[ ] Link to press assets / press kit
[ ] Review code when possible (shortly before game release or after)
[ ] PR contact info

For press kit / press asset site

[ ] Game name
[ ] Studio name
[ ] Game description / feature bullets
[ ] Planned platforms
[ ] Expected release timing
[ ] Game logo
[ ] Studio logo

[ ] Screenshots
[ ] Videos
[ ] High res art / key art (if relevant)
[ ] Press releases
[ ] PR contact info

After your game releases, you should update your web pages and online press materials with the final platforms and release dates. The updates can ensure that these resources continue to be helpful to journalists and others.

Appendix 5
Press Release Worksheet

Press Release Template / Worksheet

A press release is a formal way to announce your biggest news, using a format that's become standardized in business over the years. Brief and succinct works well (around 400–600 words.) Standard press releases include:

Headline/Subhead

Press releases start with a catchy title that communicates the most import-ant details, such as game name, genre, developer name, platforms and tim-ing. This is often followed by a subhead that provides key supplementary information, such as features, the developer's previous game(s) and so on.

Your Headline:

_____

Your Subhead:

_____

For Immediate Release

Standard "For Immediate Release" line appears at the top of press releases to communicate that this news is cleared for prompt dissemination.

Opening lines

The opening of the press release starts with the developer's location, the date the release gets distributed and the most important details of this announcement. If the reader stops reading after the first few lines, you want them to take away the gist of the news (game name, genre, plat-forms, release timeframe).

Lead lines: (Date) City—Opening lines

_____

_____

Supporting paragraphs

The next few paragraphs relay secondary information to summarize the game and establish the most important features. Include key information journalists need to know to write up a news story about the game. These paragraphs may incorporate a quote from someone in the company. Bullet points can also work well here, to help with quick reads and skimmability by busy journalists.

Additional information / details

The final paragraphs of the press release often include information such as where the game will be available and other supporting details.

Boilerplate—about (Studio)

Press releases typically end with standard boilerplate paragraphs that describe the people or companies involved. Some press releases have more than one boilerplate paragraph if multiple studios or important people are involved.

The supplementary section after Chapter 7 provides a sample press release to refer to.

Index

Page numbers in *italics* indicate a figure or table on the designated page.

announce date, marketing plan and 38–9, 60

assets *see* marketing assets

audience, target *see* target audience

auditing, marketing materials 105

awards: in marketing games 50; post-launch 136

back catalog/library of games 136–7

big announcements/reveals: in marketing plan 41–2; by press 80–4; tips for 83–4

blogs 71 *see also* website

brand bible 29

branding: brand bible 29; case study on 32–3; competitive landscape 26–7; development of 23, 25–9; differentiators 28; essential questions 25; examples of established 24; facts 25; legal side of 30; personality 26, *26*; philosophical 22–3; practical 23, 29–30; product statement 28; protecting 30; target audience 27–8

Byron, Tom 21

case studies: on branding 32–3; community development 127–9; for marketing games 53–5; for marketing plan 64–7; post-launch 138–41; for public relations 92–9

central focus of marketing materials 102–3

channels, for distributing games 11–14, 48, 61

communication channel matrix *125*

community development: 47, case study 127–9; email for 121; forums 124; initiatives 124; online video channels 124; personality and tone for 118–19; social media channels 122–3; tips 125; website for 119–21

community-driven programs: contests 135; user-generated content 135

community forums 47, 124

competitive landscape 26–7

concept art 42

Core Pitch *see* pitch statement

design and layout, of marketing material 103–5

differentiators 8, 28; marketing plan and 37

downloadable content (DLC) 134

earned media, 58–9

email: communication with press 75–8; for community development 121; mailing list 47, 121–2; press follow-up 77

events: marketing games 38–9, 48; marketing plan 42

feature, as coverage type 73

financials 13–14

forums, community *see* community forums

four "Ps" of marketing: place 12; price 11; product 11; promotion 11

game code, marketing plan 43

game support 133

guest article, as coverage type 73

hero art, in marketing plan 43

icons: do's and don'ts for 110–11; marketing materials 110

in-app purchases (IAP) 134

interview, as coverage type 72

key art, in marketing plan 43

launch date, marketing plan and 12,
  37–8, 60
legal side of branding 30
legibility, marketing material 102
library/back catalog of games 136–7

marketing fundamentals: developing
  10–13; financials and 13–14; four
  "Ps" and 11–12; game description 7–8; importance of 6; paths
  to marketplace 14–16; publisher
  vs. self-publishing 14–15; release
  timing 12–13; style of game 10;
  target audience 11; unique selling
  proposition (USP) in 9–10
marketing materials: central image
  107–8; checklists for 160–1; first
  assets of 106–8; game name/visual
  treatment 106–7; guidelines for
  102–5; icons 110; quick read 102–5;
  screenshots 109; top elements in
  108–9; updating 113; videos 109;
  view in context 112–13
marketing mix, 58–9
marketing plan: announce date
  38–9; begin thinking about 36; big
  announcements/reveals in 41–2;
  case study 64–7; developing 58–63;
  determining 36–9; launch date
  37–8; marketing mix and 59–60;
  target audience 36–7; outline for
  156–7; sample 60–1, 60; schedule
  recalibrations 62–3; sustaining plan
  61–2
marketing roadmap 40–3
media, paid/earned/owned
  58–9, 59
mini financial model 14
mission statement 28
Morganti, Emily 69

paid: marketing games 51–2; media
  58–9

personality, brand 26
philosophical, branding 22–3
pitch statement 7–8, 28–9, 76, 78
playable code, for marketing games 50
positioning statements: definition of
  8; tagline vs. 9, 9
post-launch 132–7; case study
  138–41; practical, branding 23
press 70–91; big announcements
  80–4; building a list 73–5; case
  study 92–9, consumer/pop culture/
  tech sites 71–2; email communication with 75–8; enthusiast gaming
  sites and blog 71; freelance writers
  72; mainstream gaming 71; press kit
  84; review copies 87–90; reviews/
  coverage follow-up with 132–3;
  sample media alert 81–3; specialty
  gaming 71; pitching to 78–80; types
  of 71–2; video streamers 72; when
  to talk with 85–7
press coverage: features 73; guest
  article 73; interview 72; preview 72;
  review 72–3; types of 72–3
preview, as coverage type 72
pricing 11, 49, 136
product life cycle 134–5
promotion: in marketing games
  49–50; types 49
publisher vs. self-publishing
  14–15, 15

release timing 12–13
review code 43, 87–90
reviewers, tips for 90
reviews: as coverage type 72–3;
  good reviews 89–90; tips for 88–9

sample marketing plan 60–1
schedule recalibrations 62–3
screenshots: do's and don'ts for 110;
  marketing materials 109; of marketing plan 42

seasonality, for game revenues 12
social media channels, 122–3: for
    marketing games 47
staffing: dedicated person as 17–18;
    hiring outside specialists 17; mar-
    keting person as 16–17; options for
    16–17
store pages: do's and don'ts for 112;
    marketing materials 111
sustaining plan 61–2

tagline statements, positioning
    vs. 9, 9
target audience 11; branding and
    27–8; marketing plan and 36–7

timeline, marketing 40–1
trademarking for game 29–30

unique selling proposition (USP):
    definition of 9–10
USP see unique selling proposition

videos: do's and don'ts for 110; in
    marketing games 47; marketing
    materials 109; in marketing plan 42

website: homepage 120–1; for
    marketing games 47, 51
worksheets: for marketing plan 152–4;
    press release 164–5